EVENT DESIGN

daab

Architects/Designers	Project	

INTRODUCTION

The desire to create something remarkable for a special occasion is usually the starting point of an event. Architects, designers, or specialized agencies generally develop their own versions of an effective event and compete against each other in an invitation to bid, which is called the pitch. Once an event design has been accepted, creative minds work closely with their service-providers to implement this concept. The composition of the team, fields of work, and responsibilities are readjusted for each event to meet the changing requirements. Architects, light designers, sound engineers, decorators, exhibition-booth builders, directors, and graphic artists for large events usually work in an interdisciplinary manner on solutions to problems and expand existing project ideas.

A main reference point for every concept is the space. It forms the external framework for an event, sets boundaries, or creates generous areas. All of the additional artistic elements – light, media, or decoration – are geared toward supporting the design and effect of the space. These elements are subordinate to spatial concerns, structure the existing venue, or create new areas.

Bringing together various creative disciplines into continually new areas of experience makes every event a unique occasion. When entering a new directorial territory or combining various sensory impressions sweeps the recipients away into other worlds, an event's factor of identification and experience can hardly be surpassed.

Their enormous powers of attraction combined with a deep emotional appeal make harmonious events an important aspect of business communication. They create customer loyalty or strengthen the "we feeling" of a team. The rising involvement of commercial clients and the increasing number of events illustrate their growing significance in the area of advertising.

Dependent upon the respective individually intertwined creative disciplines, each event represents an independent work. Its varied realizations and the current interest in its different types of manifestations were an important incentive for this publication. Fair and concert events, as well as strictly stage shows, are not depicted here. They are already adequately described in many other publications. The selection of the individual articles was made under consideration of a concept that has been implemented in the most complete way possible: All these projects can be perceived as a unified whole and have been consistently realized in their form, content, and creative achievement. Each event is introduced with the most important project data, together with a brief explanation, and presented in numerous pictures.

Am Anfang eines Events steht meistens der Wunsch, aus einem besonderen Anlass heraus etwas Außergewöhnliches zu schaffen. In der Regel entwickeln Architekten, Konzeptioner oder spezialisierte Agenturen ihre Version eines wirkungsvollen Events und treten in einer Ausschreibung, Pitch genannt, gegeneinander an. Hat sich ein Veranstaltungs-Entwurf durchgesetzt, arbeiten die kreativen Köpfe in enger Kooperation mit ihren Dienstleistern an der Umsetzung dieses Konzepts. Teamzusammensetzung, Arbeitsbereiche und die Verantwortlichkeiten werden für jede Veranstaltung erneut austariert, um den wechselnden Anforderungen gerecht zu werden. Architekten, Lichtdesigner, Tonmeister, Dekorateure, Messebauer, Regisseure und Grafiker arbeiten bei großen Events in der Regel interdisziplinär an Problemlösungen und vertiefen bestehende Projektideen.

Ein zentraler Bezugspunkt jeder Konzeption ist der Raum. Er bildet den äußeren Rahmen einer Veranstaltung, setzt Grenzen oder schafft großzügige Plätze. Alle weiteren gestalterischen Elemente – Licht, Medien oder Dekoration – sind darauf angelegt, die Raumgestaltung und -wirkung zu unterstützen. Sie sind den räumlichen Belangen untergeordnet, strukturieren vorhandene Örtlichkeiten oder schaffen neue Bereiche.

Die Zusammenführung verschiedener gestalterischer Disziplinen zu immer neuen Erlebnisräumen macht jeden Event zu einem einmaligen Ereignis. Wenn inszenatorisches Neuland betreten wird oder die Kombination verschiedener Sinneseindrücke den Rezipienten in andere Welten entführt, sind Identifikations- und Erlebnisfaktor eines Events kaum zu überbieten.

Ihre enorme Anziehungskraft in Verbindung mit einer tiefen emotionalen Ansprache machen stimmige Veranstaltungen zu einem wichtigen Faktor der Unternehmenskommunikation. Sie schaffen Kundenbindung oder stärken das „Wir-Gefühl" eines Teams. Das steigende Engagement der gewerblichen Auftraggeber und die zunehmende Anzahl von Events verdeutlichen ihre wachsende Bedeutung im Werbebereich.

Bedingt durch die jeweils individuell miteinander verwobenen Gestaltungsdisziplinen, stellt jeder Event ein eigenständiges Werk dar. Seine abwechslungsreichen Ausführungen und das aktuelle Interesse an seinen unterschiedlichen Erscheinungsformen waren ein wichtiger Ansporn für diese Publikation. Nicht vertreten sind Messe- und Konzertveranstaltungen sowie reine Bühnenshows. Sie werden bereits in zahlreichen anderen Veröffentlichungen ausreichend beschrieben. Die Auswahl der einzelnen Beiträge erfolgte unter Berücksichtigung eines möglichst vollständig umgesetzten Konzepts: Alle vorliegenden Projekte sind in ihrer Form, ihrem Inhalt und ihrer Kreativleistung als Einheit wahrnehmbar und wurden konsequent realisiert. Jeder Event wird mit den wichtigsten Projektdaten sowie einer kurzen Erklärung vorgestellt und in zahlreichen Bildern präsentiert.

El origen de un evento surge a menudo del deseo de crear algo extraordinario a partir de una ocasión especial. Arquitectos, creativos y agencias especializadas suelen desarrollar sus propias versiones para un determinado evento, compitiendo entre ellos al responder a un anuncio, llamado pitch. Una vez que se haya establecido el plan operativo, las fuentes creativas trabajan en estrecha cooperación con sus colaboradores en la concreta realización de los conceptos. Cada evento renueva y refresca la cohesión del equipo, los ámbitos operativos y sus correspondientes responsabilidades, todo finalizado a responder correctamente a las nuevas necesidades. Arquitectos, técnicos de luz y sonido, decoradores, constructores de stands, directores y gráficos trabajan normalmente en ocasión de los grandes eventos, buscando soluciones interdisciplinarias de los problemas y profundizando las existentes ideas creativas.

Un punto de referencia central en cada concepción es el espacio: forma el marco exterior del evento, establece fronteras o crea abundantes sitios. Todos los demás elementos formativos – luz, medios de comunicación, decoración – se organizan como consecuencia, para adaptarse a la conformación y a las funciones del espacio. Todos estos elementos quedan subordinados a las necesidades espaciales, estructurando lugares existentes o bien creando nuevas regiones.

La unificación de distintas disciplinas figurativas en experiencias espaciales cada vez más nuevas transforma cada evento en un acontecimiento único, y si descubrimos nuevas posibilidades escénicas o si la combinación de diversos estímulos sensoriales transporta el observador en otros mundos, es difícil sobreestimar los factores de identificación y experimentación.

El enorme atractivo que ejercen estos factores, junto con su profundo mensaje emocional, hacen que una harmónica disposición espacial sea un factor importante en la comunicación empresarial. Este aspecto crea el vínculo con el cliente o refuerza la sensación de pertenencia a "nuestro" equipo. El progresivo compromiso por parte de los clientes comerciales y la creciente cantidad de eventos clarifican el significado de estos factores en el mundo de la publicidad.

Dependiendo de la interrelación de las varias disciplinas figurativas individuales, cada evento representa una obra única e independiente. Las diversas realizaciones y el interés corriente para las distintas formas expresivas han sido un estímulo importante para esta publicación. No se incluyen ferias ni conciertos, ni tampoco puras representaciones escénicas, puesto que éstas ya están suficientemente descritas en numerosas otras publicaciones. La selección de cada contribución sigue la consideración de conceptos de conversión lo más completa posible: todos los proyectos considerados tienen la capacidad de ser percibidos en su forma, contenido e impacto creativo, y han sido realizados en consecuencia. Cada evento es presentado junto con los principales datos proyectuales y con una breve descripción, e ilustrado por medio de numerosas imágenes.

Le désir de créer quelque chose de remarquable pour une occasion particulière est généralement le point de départ d'un événement. Les architectes, les designers ou les agences spécialisées mettent généralement au point leur propre version de l'événement et rivalisent lors de l'appel d'offre, qu'on appelle le pitch. Une fois qu'un concept événementiel a été accepté, les esprits créatifs travaillent étroitement avec leurs fournisseurs de service pour mettre ce concept en œuvre. La composition de l'équipe, les domaines de travail et les responsabilités sont ajustés à chaque événement pour se conformer à des exigences changeantes. Architectes, concepteurs lumière, ingénieurs du son, décorateurs, constructeurs de boxes, metteurs en scène et graphistes des grands événements travaillent généralement de manière interdisciplinaire pour trouver des solutions aux problèmes et développer les idées de projet préexistantes.

Le point de référence majeur de chaque concept est l'espace. Il forme le cadre externe de l'événement, définit des limites ou crée des espaces généreux. Tous les éléments artistiques traditionnels – lumière, médias, ou décoration – sont développés ensemble pour renforcer le design et les effets de l'espace. Ces éléments sont subordonnés aux questions spatiales, ils structurent l'espace existant, ou créent de nouvelles zones.

Le fait de réunir diverses disciplines créatives dans des champs d'expérience continuellement renouvelés fait de chaque événement une occasion unique. En entrant dans un nouveau territoire de mise en scène ou en combinant des impressions sensorielles variées, on envoie les spectateurs vers d'autres mondes ; le facteur identification, l'expérience d'un événement, peuvent difficilement être surpassés.

Ce fantastique pouvoir d'attraction, lié à un profond attrait émotionnel, fait d'un événement harmonieux un aspect important de la communication commerciale. Il crée une fidélité chez le consommateur ou renforce le « sentiment d'appartenance » d'une équipe. L'implication grandissante des clients et le nombre croissant d'événements illustrent leur signification de plus en plus importante dans le domaine de la publicité.

Bien que dépendant des différentes disciplines créatives associées, chaque événement est une œuvre indépendante. Les réalisations variées et l'intérêt actuel pour les différents types de manifestations sont les principales raisons de cette publication. Les foires et les concerts, tout comme les spectacles au sens strict, ne sont pas représentés ici. Ils ont déjà suffisamment été décrits dans de nombreux autres ouvrages. Chacun des articles a été sélectionné parce qu'il montrait un concept mis en œuvre de la manière la plus complète possible : tous ces projets peuvent être perçus comme un tout unifié et ont été réalisés de manière cohérente dans leur forme, leur fond, d'où leur réussite créative. Chaque événement est présenté avec les données majeures du projet, accompagnées d'une brève explication, et est illustré de nombreuses images.

All'origine di un evento si trova spesso il desiderio di tirare fuori qualcosa di straordinario da un'occasione speciale. Generalmente sono gli architetti, i creativi o le agenzie specializzate i responsabili dello sviluppo di un evento efficace, rispondendo a un annuncio, chiamato pitch, ed entrando in competizione tra loro. Una volta stabilito un piano operativo, le menti creative lavorano in stretta cooperazione con i loro collaboratori alla realizzazione pratica dei concetti. Ogni manifestazione rinnova la coesione di squadra, le rispettive aree di lavoro e responsabilità, in modo da rispondere correttamente alle mutevoli necessità. Architetti, designer dell'illuminazione, tecnici del suono, decoratori, standisti, registi e grafici collaborano regolarmente alla soluzione in ambito interdisciplinare dei problemi legati ai grossi eventi, approfondendo i concetti progettuali già presenti.

Un punto di riferimento fondamentale di ogni ideazione è lo spazio: determina la struttura esterna dell'evento, ne stabilisce i confini o crea posti in abbondanza. Tutti gli altri elementi figurativi – luci, multimedialità, decorazione – vengono sistemati in modo da seguire la conformazione e la funzionalità dello spazio: sono subordinati alle esigenze spaziali, conferiscono struttura a ubicazioni già esistenti o creano nuovi ambiti.

L'unificazione di discipline figurative differenti in esperienze spaziali sempre nuove trasforma ogni evento in un avvenimento unico. Se intervengono terreni scenici inesplorati, o se la combinazione di diversi stimoli sensoriali trasporta l'osservatore in altri mondi, ecco che i fattori identificativi e sperimentativi dell'evento non possono più essere sottovalutati.

L'enorme potere attrattivo di questi fattori, collegato con il profondo messaggio emozionale, fanno di un'armoniosa organizzazione spaziale un fattore importante per la comunicazione aziendale, costruendo il legame con il cliente o rafforzando il senso di appartenenza alla squadra. Il crescente impegno da parte dei committenti e il costante aumento del numero di eventi testimoniano il significato di questi fattori nel mondo della pubblicità.

Condizionato dalle singole discipline figurative sempre intrecciate tra di loro, ciascun evento rappresenta un'opera a sé stante. Le realizzazioni ricche di varietà e l'attuale interesse per le differenti forme espressive hanno costituito un importante stimolo per questa pubblicazione. Si è scelto di non presentare eventi fieristici e concertistici, così come pure rappresentazioni sceniche, visto che questi avvenimenti sono già sufficientemente descritti in numerose altre pubblicazioni. La selezione dei singoli contributi è basata sulla considerazione di un concetto di conversione per quanto possibile completa: tutti i progetti considerati sono percettibili come unità nella loro forma, nel loro contenuto e nel loro effetto creativo, e sono stati realizzati di conseguenza. Ogni evento è presentato insieme ai principali dati progettuali e a una breve descrizione, e illustrato tramite numerose immagini.

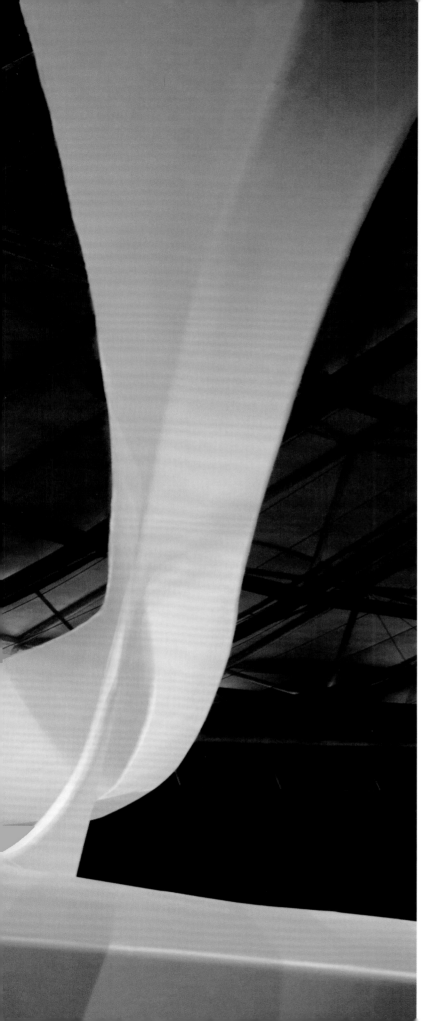

3DELUXE | WIESBADEN
OC 2006 FIFA World Cup, Closing Ceremony
Berlin, Germany | 9 July 2006
Photos: 3deluxe, Christian Bauer, Emanuel Raab

At the closing celebration of the 2006 World Soccer Cup, the curved form of the stage structures contrasted with the monolithic architecture of Marathon Gate at the Berlin Olympic Stadium. The production included about 200 performers such as drummers, dancers, and standard-bearers. More than 60 participants waved textile umbrella with a green-white motif that pointed in an abstract form to lawns and field lines—the main site of the World Cup.

Bei der Abschlussfeier der Fußball-WM 2006 kontrastierte die geschwungene Form der Bühnenbauten mit der monolithischen Architektur des Marathontors im Berliner Olympiastadion. In die Inszenierung waren rund 200 Darsteller, darunter Trommler, Tänzer und Fahnenträgerinnen eingebunden. Über 60 Akteure schwenkten textile Schirme, deren grün-weißes Motiv in abstrakter Form auf Rasen und Feldlinien verwies – den Hauptschauplatz der WM.

En la ceremonia de clausura del Mundial de Fútbol de 2006 contrastaron las sinuosas formas del escenario con la arquitectura monolítica de la Puerta de Maratón del Estadio Olímpico de Berlín. En el montaje participaron unos 200 artistas, incluyendo percusionistas, bailarines y portadores de banderas. Más de 60 actores se encargaron de agitar unas pantallas circulares de tela con motivos abstractos en verde y blanco, como el campo y sus líneas divisorias: el escenario principal del Mundial.

Lors de la cérémonie de clôture de la Coupe du Monde 2006, la forme courbe des structures scéniques contrastait avec l'architecture monolithique du Marathon Gate du Stade Olympique de Berlin. Le spectacle comprenait plus de 200 artistes, batteurs, danseurs et porte-drapeaux. Plus de 60 participants agitaient des écrans textiles avec un motif vert et blanc, qui désignaient dans une forme abstraite les pelouses et les lignes du terrain – le site principal de la Coupe du Monde.

Durante i festeggiamenti per la fine dei Campionati Mondiali di calcio 2006 la forma arcuata delle costruzioni sul palcoscenico rappresentava un contrasto con l'architettura monolitica della porta della maratona nello stadio olimpico di Berlino. Nella rappresentazione erano presenti 200 interpreti, tra i quali dei suonatori di tamburo, ballerini e ragazze portabandiera. Oltre 60 attori hanno sventolato schermi tessili che con i loro motivi verde-bianco rimandavano in forma astratta al prato e alle linee di campo – la scena principale dei Campionati Mondiali.

3DELUXE | WIESBADEN
LIGHTLIFE | COLOGNE
Artevent GmbH, "Fußball Globus"
World Cup host cities, Germany | 2003-2006
Photos: Emanuel Raab, Wolfgang Stahl

Jules Rimet Trophäe,
wurde der Deutschen Nationalmannschaft
im Jahre 195.. zum Gewinn der FIFA

The Soccer Globe combines the image of the globe with the form of the soccer ball. During its three-year tour through the 12 World Cup cities, its guests were able to get involved with the topic of soccer in an emotional and playful way. The exhibited cult objects of the soccer sport, as well as interactive installations with which the visitors became the players on the field, served this purpose.

Der Fußball Globus verknüpfte das Bild der Weltkugel mit der Form des Fußballs. Während seiner dreijährigen Tournee durch die 12 WM-Städte konnten sich seine Gäste auf emotionale und spielerische Weise mit dem Thema Fußball befassen. Ausgestellte Kultobjekte des Fußballsports dienten dazu ebenso wie interaktive Installationen, mit denen die Besucher selbst zu Akteuren auf dem Spielfeld wurden.

El Globo Esférico aunó la imagen del globo terráqueo y la forma de un balón de fútbol. Durante los tres años que estuvo de gira por las 12 sedes del Mundial de Fútbol, sus visitantes pudieron ver el fútbol desde una perspectiva emocional y lúdica a través de los objetos de culto del mundo del fútbol allí expuestos y de las instalaciones interactivas, con las que los presentes se convirtieron en actores en el terreno de juego.

Le Globe du Football combine l'image du globe avec la forme du ballon de football. Pendant sa tournée de trois années à travers les 12 villes de la Coupe du Monde, les visiteurs pouvaient s'impliquer de manière ludique et émouvante sur le thème du football. Les expositions d'objets cultes du football, ainsi que les installations interactives grâce auxquelles les visiteurs devenaient les joueurs sur le terrain, ont été conçues dans ce but.

Il Globo del calcio ha collegato l'immagine del globo terrestre con la forma del pallone da calcio. Durante la sua tournée, durata tre anni attraverso 12 città dei mondiali di calcio, i suoi ospiti si sono potuti occupare del tema del calcio in modo emozionale e giocoso. A questo scopo sono serviti degli oggetti di culto dello sport calcistico esposti e installazioni interattive, con i quali i visitatori stessi potevano diventare attori sul campo di gioco.

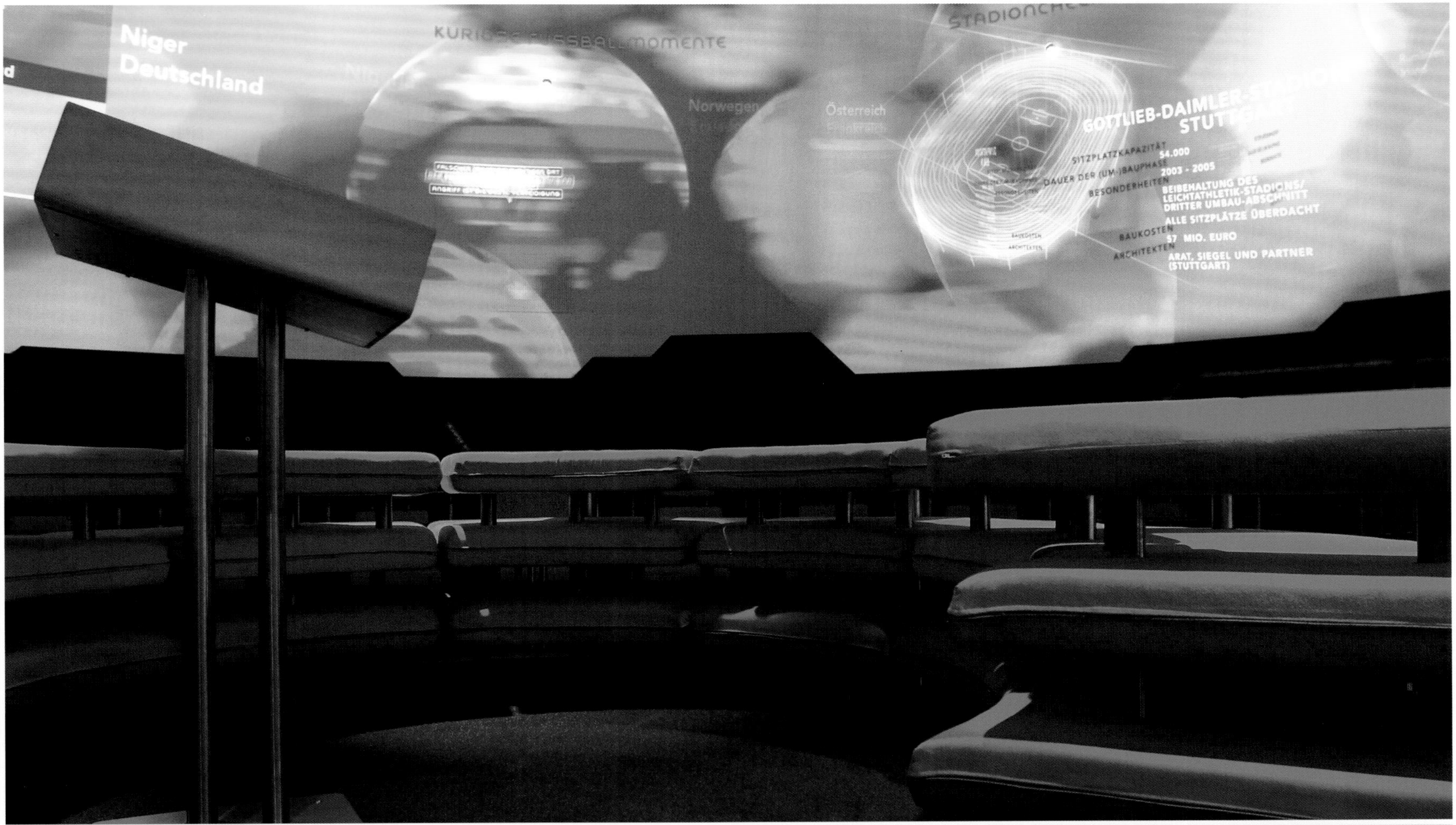
Niger
Deutschland
Norwegen
Österreich
SITZPLATZKAPAZITÄT
54.000
DAUER DER (UM-)BAUPHASE
2003 - 2005
BESONDERHEITEN
BEIBEHALTUNG DES LEICHTATHLETIK-STADIONS/
DRITTER UMBAU-ABSCHNITT
ALLE SITZPLÄTZE ÜBERDACHT
BAUKOSTEN
57 MIO. EURO
ARCHITEKTEN
ARAT, SIEGEL UND PARTNER
(STUTTGART)

TORWART-SPIEL
FUSSBALL - MEINE LIEBE
WILLKOMMEN IM FUSSBALL GLOBUS
Ich liebe Fussball, weil _

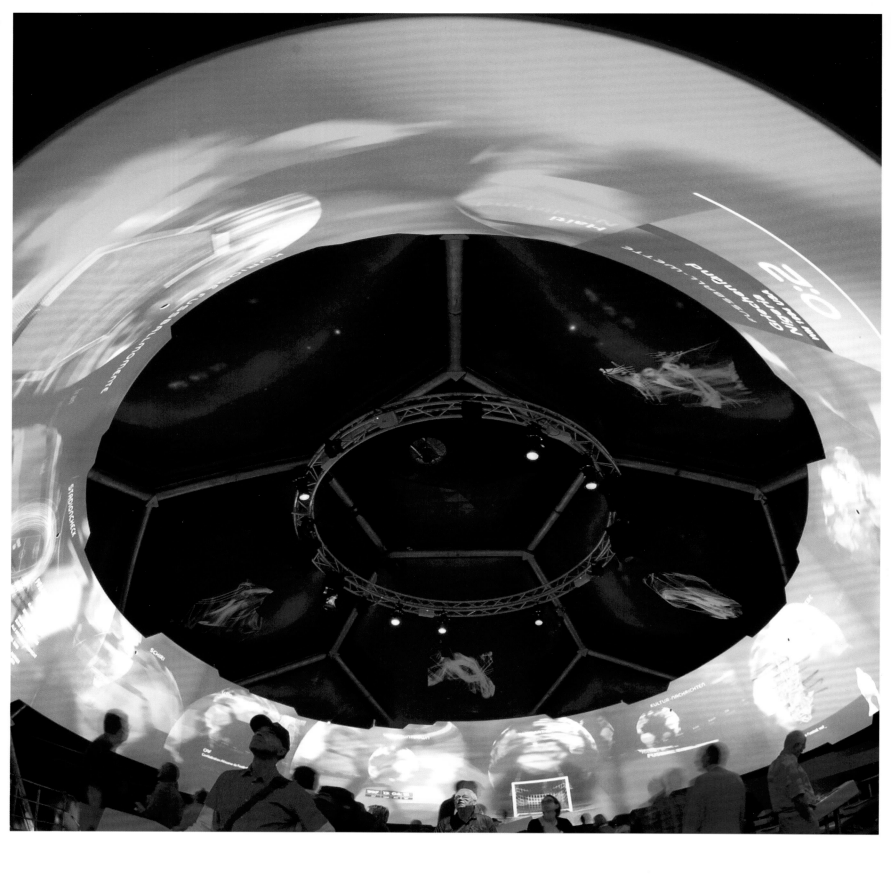

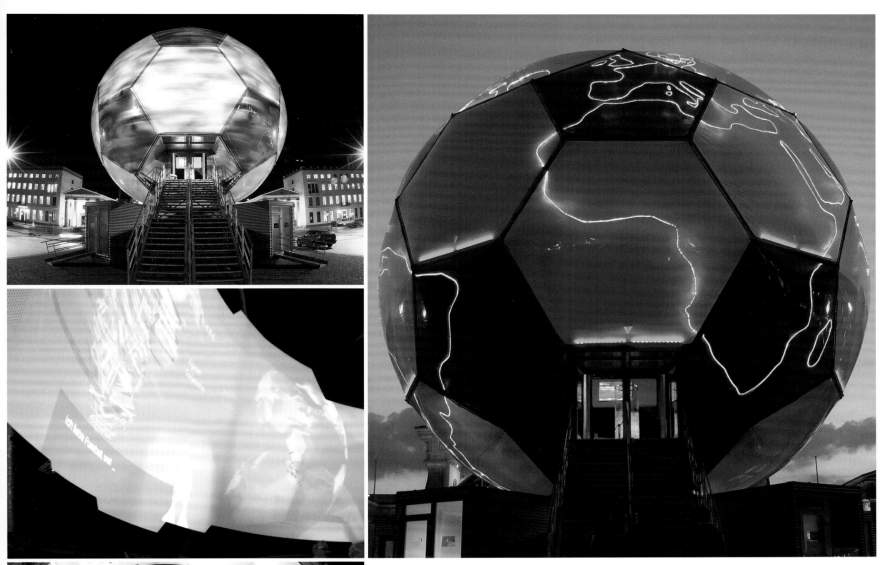
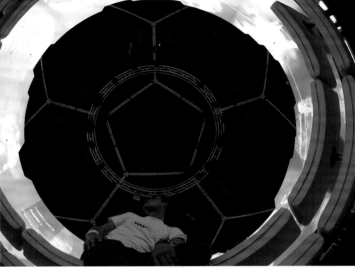

ATELIER MARKGRAPH | FRANKFURT
Tourismus+Congress GmbH Frankfurt am Main
ART | WHEEL—Museum Riverbank Festival
Frankfurt am Main, Germany | 26 - 28 August 2005
Photos: Amir Molana, Cem Yücetas

With the Frankfurt skyline as the stage setting, the KUNST|RAD (art wheel) served as a platform for the museums of the Rhine-Main region at the 2005 Museum Bank Festival. With its height of 131 feet, the ferries wheel with lights and media recorded on it offered a journey through the epochs, styles, and colors as it introduced 100 masterpieces from 16 museums. As a globe, the wheel ultimately became the symbol for the international cultural world of Frankfurt.

Mit der Frankfurter Skyline als Bühnenbild diente das KUNST|RAD beim Museumsuferfest 2005 als Plattform für die Museen der Rhein-Main-Region. Mit seiner Höhe von 40 Metern bot das mit Licht und Medien bespielte Riesenrad eine Fahrt durch Epochen, Stile und Farben und stellte 100 Meisterwerke aus 16 Museen vor. Als Weltkugel wurde das Rad schließlich zum Sinnbild der internationalen Kulturwelt Frankfurts.

Con la silueta de los rascacielos de Fráncfort como telón de fondo, la KUNST|RAD (noria del arte) del Festival de los Museos de la Ribera de 2005 sirvió de escaparate a los museos de la región del Rhin-Meno. Las proyecciones sobre esta noria de 40 metros de altura ofrecieron un viaje por distintas épocas, estilos y colores y presentaron 100 obras de 16 museos. En forma de globo terráqueo, la noria simbolizó el cosmopolita mundo cultural de Fráncfort.

Avec la silhouette de Francfort comme décor, la KUNST|RAD (Roue d'Art) a servi de plateforme pour les musées de la région Rhin-Main lors de la Fête des musées 2005. Haute de 40 mètres, cette grande roue ornée de supports médias et de lumières proposait un voyage à travers les époques, les styles et les couleurs en présentant 100 chefs d'œuvres provenant de 16 musées. Représentant par un globe, la roue est ensuite devenue le symbole du monde culturel international de Francfort.

Con la skyline di Francoforte come scenografia la KUNST|RAD (ruota artistica) al festival dei musei sulle rive 2005 ha avuto funzione di piattaforma per i musei della regione Reno-Meno. Con la sua altezza di 40 metri la ruota panoramica riempita di luci e media ha offerto un viaggio attraverso epoche, stili e colori, e ha presentato 100 opere d'arte tratte da 16 musei. Nell'assumere la forma di un globo terrestre infine la ruota è diventata il simbolo del mondo culturale internazionale di Francoforte.

ATELIER MARKGRAPH | FRANKFURT
Tourismus+Congress GmbH Frankfurt am Main
MainArena—Public Viewing Area for World Championship
Frankfurt, Germany | 9 June - 9 July 2006
Photos: Nina Siber, Jürgen Blumenthal

At the 2006 Soccer World Cup, Frankfurt am Main invited people to a gigantic public stadium: the MainArena. Two huge LED screens were anchored into the ground with pillars measuring many yards at the Main River for the broadcasting of the World Cup games to both sides of the bank. With a picture surface of 483 sq. ft. each, they were the largest video walls used for the World Cup and turned the game broadcasts into a shared experience.

Zur Fußball-WM 2006 lud Frankfurt am Main in ein gigantisches öffentliches Stadion: die MainArena. Für die Übertragung der WM-Spiele auf beide Uferseiten wurden zwei riesige LED-Flächen mit meterlangen Pfeilern im Grund des Mains verankert. Mit jeweils 144 m² Bildfläche waren es die größten Videowände, die bei der WM zum Einsatz kamen; und machten so die Ausstrahlung der Spiele zum Gemeinschaftserlebnis.

Durante el Mundial de fútbol de 2006, Fráncfort invitó a todo el mundo a un gigantesco estadio público: el MainArena (el "estadio del Meno"). Para las retransmisiones de los partidos en ambas orillas, se instalaron dos pantallas enormes fijadas al lecho del río con unos larguísimos pilares. Con sus 144 m² de superficie, fueron las más grandes de todo el Mundial y convirtieron las retransmisiones en una experiencia colectiva.

Pendant la Coupe du Monde de Football 2006, Francfort-sur-le-Main invitait les visteurs dans un immense stade public : le MainArena. Pour la retransmission des matches de chaque côté de la rivière, deux immenses surfaces DEL étaient ancrées dans le sol sur des piliers de plusieurs mètres de haut. Avec un écran d'une surface de 144 m² chacun, c'étaient les plus grands murs vidéo utilisés pendant la Coupe du Monde et ils ont permis de faire de la diffusion des matches une expérience partagée.

In occasione dei campionati mondiali di calcio 2006 Francoforte ha invitato i suoi ospiti in un gigantesco stadio aperto al pubblico: la MainArena. Per la trasmissione dei campionati del mondo su tutte e due le sponde sono stati ancorate due enormi superfici LED tramite pilastri lunghi svariati metri nel suolo del fiume Meno. Con schermi ognuno da 144 m² essi si sono aggiudicati il primato delle pareti a video più grandi che siano state adoperate per i campionati del mondo e hanno fatto sì che la trasmissione delle partite si trasformasse in un evento collettivo.

ATELIER MARKGRAPH | FRANKFURT
Tourismus+Congress GmbH Frankfurt am Main
Ship of Ideas
Frankfurt, Germany | 29 - 31 August 2003
Photos: Katja Hoffmann

The "Ship of Ideas" made a statement for the 2003 Museum Bank Festival in Frankfurt as a sign of the region's cultural wealth. After nightfall, the ship glided—as a floating cuboid of screens and LEDs illuminated with light and projections—for 45 minutes along the Main River and gave the festival visitors insights into the expositions and cultural treasures of the museums as it passed them.

Das „Schiff der Ideen" setzte auf dem Museumsuferfest in Frankfurt 2003 ein Zeichen für den Kulturreichtum der Region. Nach Einbruch der Dunkelheit glitt das Schiff – ein schwimmender, mit Licht und Projektionen illuminierter Quader aus Leinwänden und LEDs – 45 Minuten lang über den Main und gab den Festbesuchern Einblicke in die Expositionen und Kulturschätze der Museen, an denen es vorüberzog.

El "bajel de las ideas" simbolizó la riqueza cultural de la región durante el Festival de los Museos de la Ribera de Fráncfort en 2003. Al caer la noche, las proyecciones sobre pantallas y rótulos de diodos de este poliedro flotante en el río Meno brillaban durante 45 minutos, y a su paso ofrecía a los visitantes información sobre las exposiciones y los tesoros culturales de los museos.

Le « Bateau des Idées » est apparu en 2003 à la Fête des Musées de Francfort comme le symbole de la richesse culturelle de la région. A la tombée de la nuit, ce bateau glissait – comme un cube d'écrans et de DEL flottant, illuminé de lumières et de projection – pendant 45 minutes le long du Main et donnait aux visiteurs du festival un aperçu des expositions et des trésors culturels des musées.

La „nave delle idee" ha lasciato il segno al festival dei musei sulle rive di Francoforte 2003 per la ricchezza culturale della regione. All'imbrunire la nave – un quadrato fatto di tele e di LED che galleggiava illuminato da luci e proiezioni – è scivolato per 45 minuti sul Meno permettendo ai visitatori della festa di dare uno sguardo alle esposizioni e ai tesori culturali dei musei accanto ai quali stava passando.

AUDITOIRE | PARIS
Orange—France Telecom, Orange Rebranding
Paris, France | June 2006
Photos: © David Lefranc, Evelyne Garat,
Philippe Jacob, Raphaël Soret

France Telekom celebrated the grouping of its cell-phone, internet, and television activities under the sole brand of Orange—which creates the possibility of opening up to other markets—with numerous events. Street promotions took place in more than 42 cities. The finale was a large party on the terrace of Saint Cloud Park with a view of Paris. Dominating color: orange.

Die Gruppierung ihrer Mobilfunk-, Internet- und Fernsehaktivitäten unter der alleinigen Marke "Orange" mit der Möglichkeit der Öffnung hin zu anderen Märkten feierte die France Telecom mit zahlreichen Events. In über 42 Städten fanden Straßenaktionen statt. Den Abschluss bildete eine große Party auf der Terrasse des Saint-Cloud-Parks mit Blick über Paris. Dominierende Farbe: orange.

La France Telecom celebró con numerosos actos la unificación de sus divisiones de telefonía móvil, Internet y televisión en una sola marca, "Orange", abriéndose así la posibilidad de penetrar en otros mercados. En más de 42 ciudades se realizaron promociones por las calles. El colofón lo puso una gran fiesta en la terraza del parque de Saint Cloud con vistas a París. El color dominante fue el naranja.

France Telecom a célébré le regroupement de ses activités de téléphonie mobile, Internet et télévision sous la marque unique Orange – ce qui lui permet de s'ouvrir à d'autres marchés – en organisant de nombreuses manifestations. Des opérations promotionnelles ont eu lieu dans les rues de plus de 42 villes. Un final avec une grande soirée festive surplombant Paris au Domaine National du Parc de Saint Cloud. Couleur dominante : orange.

La France Telecom ha festeggiato con numerosi eventi il raggruppamento delle sue attività di telefonia mobile, Internet e televisione sotto il marchio unico "Orange" con la possibilità di apertura verso altri mercati. In più di 42 città hanno avuto luogo degli spettacoli in strada. La conclusione è stata offerta da una grande festa sul terrazzo del Domaine National du Parc de Saint Cloud con vista su Parigi. Il colore dominante: l'arancione.

AUDITOIRE | PARIS
Philips, "Aurea" Launch
Paris, France | June 2007
Photos: © Alain Pérus, Myli Bourigault
& Eloïse Bollack - L'Œil du Diaph

Philips celebrated the launch of its new Aurea Flat TV in the renowned Paris club Showcase under the Alexandre III bridge. The 700 guests were seduced into an immersive viewing experience of the new TV, set in a luxurious ambience that was inspired by Philips partnerships across different creative fields: cinema, embodied by director Wong Kar Wai; fashion photography, by famous Vogue photographer Vincent Peters as well as fashion with the Lanvin brand.

Philips zelebrierte die Einführung seines neuen Aurea Flat TV im renommierten Pariser Club „Showcase" unter der Brücke Alexandre III. Die 700 Gäste wurden dazu verführt, in eine revolutionäre Erfahrung des Fernsehens einzutauchen. Initiiert im luxuriösen Ambiente und inspiriert von Philips fachgebietsübergreifenden Partnerschaften: mit dem Kino, verkörpert durch Regisseur Wong Kar Wai, der Modephotographie des berühmten Voguefotografen Vincent Peters sowie der Mode der Marke Lanvin.

Philips celebró la salida al mercado de su nuevo monitor de LCD "Aurea" en el afamado club parisino "Showcase" bajo el Puente de Alejandro III. Los 700 invitados disfrutaron de una experiencia revolucionaria en un ambiente de lujo para conocer el nuevo monitor. Para ello, Philips se sirvió de disciplinas como el cine, teniendo al director Wong Kar Wai como representante, la fotografía de moda del célebre Vogue fotógrafo Vincent Peters, y la propia moda a cargo de la firma Lanvin.

Philips a célébré le lancement de son nouveau téléviseur LCD « Aurea » au Showcase, nouveau club parisien sous le pont Alexandre III. Les 700 invités ont pu se laisser séduire par le nouveau téléviseur et sa technologie dans une atmosphère luxueuse inspirée par deux univers créatifs forts : le cinéma, incarné par le réalisateur Wong Kar Wai, la photographie de mode avec le célèbre photographe de Vogue, Vincent Peters, et enfin la mode avec Lanvin.

Philips ha celebrato il lancio della sua nuova TV Aurea Flat nel rinomato Club parigino „Showcase" sotto il ponte Alexandre III. I 700 invitati sono stati sedotti ad immergersi in una esperienza rivoluzionaria del mondo della televisione. Promossa nel lussuoso ambiente ed ispirata dalla Philips tramite partner prossimi al settore: il cinema, impersonato dal regista Wong Kar Wai e la fotografia di moda grazie al fotografo di Vogue Vincent Peters e la moda di Lanvin.

AUDITOIRE | PARIS
SNCF, The Great TGV 25th anniversary celebration
Paris, France | 2006
Photos: © Arnaud Lamolie

The TGV was the first European high-speed train and was inaugurated on the route between Paris and Lyon in 1981. Since then, TGV has become a national symbol for the French, who celebrated it with 25 small events throughout 2006. The celebration reached its climax with an event in honour of TGV's 25th anniversary: a TGV was driven in front of the Eiffel Tower and the Palais de Chaillot and put in the limelight for two nights with a light and sound show.

Der TGV ist der erste europäische Hochgeschwindigkeitszug und wurde 1981 auf der Strecke von Paris nach Lyon eingeführt. Seitdem ist der Zug für die Franzosen ein nationales Symbol geworden. Deshalb war das Jahr 2006 von 25 kleineren Events begleitet. Höhepunkt war aber die große 25-Jahr-Feier: Ein TGV wurde vor den Eiffelturm und das Palais de Chaillot gefahren und zwei Nächte lang mit einer Licht- und Soundshow in Szene gesetzt.

El TGV fue el primer tren europeo de alta velocidad y circuló por primera vez entre París y Lyon en 1981. Desde entonces, el TGV se ha convertido en Francia en un símbolo nacional que se ha celebrado con 25 eventos a lo largo del 2006. La celebración culminó con los festejos del 25 aniversario: un TGV delante de la Torre Eiffel y del Palacio de Chaillot protagonizó un espectáculo de luz y sonido durante dos noches.

Le premier train à grande vitesse européen est un TGV. La première circulation a été inaugurée en 1981 sur la ligne Paris/Lyon. Ce train est devenu un symbole national français. Ainsi 2006 a vu se dérouler une série de 25 événements tout au long de l'année. L'apothéose fut la célébration majeure du 25ème anniversaire durant deux jours et deux nuits, une rame TGV au pied de la Tour Eiffel devant le Palais de Chaillot en vedette avec un spectacle son et lumière.

Il TGV è stato il primo treno ad alta velocità Europeo e fu inaugurato nel 1981 sulla tratta Parigi/Lione. Da allora, è diventato un simbolo nazionale per i Francesi che lo hanno celebrato con 25 piccoli eventi durante tutto il 2006. Il momento culminante della celebrazione è stato l'evento organizzato per il venticinquesimo anniversario: un TGV davanti alla torre Eiffel ed al Palais de Chaillot è stato il protagonista di uno spettacolo di luci e suoni per due notti.

AUDITOIRE | PARIS
Renault, Twingo Live
Paris, France | 2007
Photos: Viviane Negrotto, Nicolas Chauveau

Renault presented the New Twingo in Stade de France near Paris to about 10,000 dealers. The show with a variety of acts in the curve of the stadium lasted an entire day: Dance performances, bands, and DJs entertained the guests; a type of ballet with cars displayed the Twingo in its three facets of feisty, practical and connected. Gigantic screens with a total of 656 sq. ft. supported the presentation.

Vor rund 10.000 Händlern präsentierte Renault den Neuen Twingo im Stade de France bei Paris. Einen ganzen Tag lang dauerte die abwechslungsreiche Show in der Kurve des Stadions: Tanzvorführungen, Bands und DJs unterhielten die Gäste; eine Art Ballett mit Autos zeigte den Twingo in seinen drei Facetten von lebhaft, praktisch und verbunden. Riesige Leinwände mit insgesamt 200 m² Fläche unterstützten die Präsentation.

Renault presentó su Nuevo Twingo en el Stade de France de París ante unos 10.000 distribuidores. Un día entero se extendió el variado espectáculo celebrado en una de las curvas del estadio. Los asistentes se divirtieron con las actuaciones de bailarines, grupos musicales y dj's. Las tres versiones del Twingo -Feisty, Practical y Connected- se presentaron con un ballet, respaldado por unas pantallas gigantes con un total de 200 m².

Renault a présenté la Nouvelle Twingo au Stade de France, près de Paris, à environ 10 000 vendeurs. Le show comprenait diverses parties dans l'enceinte du stade et a duré un jour entier : démonstrations de danse, orchestre live et DJ pour divertir les invités. Un ballet de véhicules a dévoilé la nouvelle Twingo sous ses trois facettes : tonique, pratique et branchée. Un dispositif d'écrans géants d'une surface totale de 200 m² venait soutenir le show.

Renault ha presentato davanti a circa 10.000 venditori la Nuova Twingo nello Stade de France presso Parigi. Lo spettacolo vario, rappresentato nella curva dello stadio, è durato un giorno intero: rappresentazioni di balletti, bande e DJ hanno intrattenuto gli ospiti; un tipo di Balletto con delle macchine ha mostrato la Twingo nelle sue tre sfaccettature altezzosa, pratica e coerente. Enormi schermi con complessivi 200 m² di superficie hanno supportato la presentazione.

AVCOMMUNICATION GMBH | LUDWIGSBURG
BSH Bosch und Siemens Hausgeräte GmbH
product presentation & exhibition
Duisburg, Germany | 2007
Photos: Sabine Lubenow

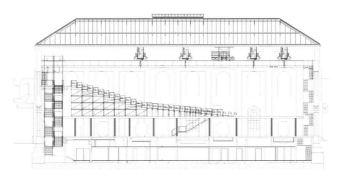

With a lavish production, the Bosch und Siemens Hausgeräte GmbH introduced a new series in the Duisburg Landschaftspark (landscape park). The leitmotif was the element of "water": Acoustic effects, interactive projections, as well as a real waterfall created the impressive backdrop of the event. In an extensive exhibition, the brands of the BSH Group presented their new appliances within individual furnishings, but always in a uniform cubic white language of form.

Mit einer aufwendigen Inszenierung stellte die Bosch und Siemens Hausgeräte GmbH eine neue Baureihe im Landschaftspark Duisburg vor. Leitmotiv war das Element „Wasser": Akustische Effekte, interaktive Projektionen sowie ein realer Wasserfall schufen die beeindruckende Kulisse der Veranstaltung. In einer umfassenden Ausstellung präsentierten die Marken der BSH-Gruppe ihre neuen Geräte in individuellem Mobiliar, stets aber in einer einheitlich kubisch weißen Formensprache.

Con una suntuosa puesta en escena presentó Bosch und Siemens Hausgeräte GmbH su nueva línea en el parque Landschaftspark de Duisburg. El leitmotiv fue el agua: efectos sonoros, proyecciones interactivas y una verdadera cascada constituyeron el telón de fondo del espectáculo. En una grandiosa exposición, las marcas del grupo BSH presentaron en stands individualizados sus nuevos aparatos, si bien todos ellos eran de color blanco y compartían las mismas formas cúbicas.

Avec une mise en scène grandiose, Bosch und Siemens Hausgeräte GmbH a présenté une nouvelle collection dans le Duisburg Landschaftspark. Le leitmotiv en était l'élément « eau » : des effets acoustiques, des projections interactives, ainsi qu'une véritable cascade formaient l'impressionnant cadre de l'événement. Dans une exposition exhaustive, les marques du groupe BSH présentaient leurs nouveaux appareils avec des prestations différenciées, mais toujours dans un langage formel blanc cubique et uniforme.

Attraverso un allestimento impegnativo la Bosch und Siemens Hausgeräte GmbH presentato una nuova serie di prodotti nel parco paesaggistico di Duisburg. Il Leitmotiv è stato l'elemento „acqua": gli effetti acustici, le proiezioni interattive oltre a una vera cascata hanno creato lo scenario impressionante della rappresentazione. In una vasta mostra le marche del gruppo BSH hanno presentato i loro elettrodomestici con un mobilio individuale, ma sempre in un linguaggio di forme bianche e cubiche unitarie.

BLUE SCOPE COMMUNICATIONS | BERLIN
BMW AG, BMW X5 Dealer Drive Event
BMW CleanEnergy Valencia
Valencia, Spain | February/March 2007
Photos: Katja Hoffmann

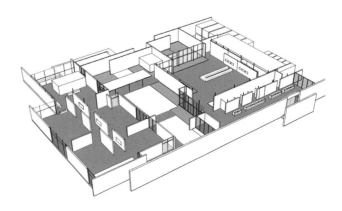

The BMW CleanEnergy Station was the surprising highlight of the BMW Dealer Drive Events in Valencia. Dealers were given the exclusive opportunity of driving a BMW Hydrogen 7 that is powered by hydrogen. The common intersection of a more coolly designed, technically oriented exhibition and an atmospherically warmer dialog and service zone was the vehicle exhibition area that united the presumed opposites.

Die BMW CleanEnergy Station war das überraschende Highlight des BMW Dealer Drive Events in Valencia. Händler konnten exklusiv einen mit Wasserstoff betriebenen BMW Hydrogen 7 fahren. Gemeinsame Schnittmenge einer kühler gestalteten, technisch orientierten Ausstellung und einer atmosphärisch wärmeren Dialog- und Servicezone war die Fahrzeugausstellungsfläche, die vermeintliche Gegensätze vereinte.

La Estación de Energía Limpia de BMW (la "Clean Energy Station") fue lo más destacado de las Jornadas de Conducción para Distribuidores que BMW celebró en Valencia. Estos tuvieron la oportunidad de conducir un BMW 7 propulsado por hidrógeno. La exposición fusionaba en espacios compartidos su carácter técnico y su fría concepción con la calidez de la zona de servicio y comunicación para aunar así extremos supuestamente antagónicos.

La CleanEnergy Station BMW était le surprenant point d'orgue du BMW Dealer Drive Events à Valence. Les vendeurs se sont vu accorder la chance exclusive de conduire la BMW Hydrogen 7, propulsée à l'hydrogène. L'intersection entre une exposition au design plus froid, orientée vers la technique, et un espace de service et de dialogue plus chaud, était la zone d'exposition des véhicules qui unissait ces présumés opposés.

La stazione BMW CleanEnergy è stata il culmine sorprendente degli eventi del BMW Dealer Drive a Valencia. I venditori hanno potuto guidare in esclusiva la BMW Hydrogen 7 funzionante a idrogeno. Un insieme d'intersezione di una mostra freddamente realizzata e orientata tecnicamente e una zona di dialogo e di assistenza di atmosfera più calda: questa è stata la superficie di esposizione della vettura che ha unito delle presunte contraddizioni.

BLUE SCOPE COMMUNICATIONS | BERLIN
BMW AG, BMW X5 Dealer Drive Event
BMW Terminal Valencia
Valencia, Spain | February/March 2007
Photos: diephotodesigner.de

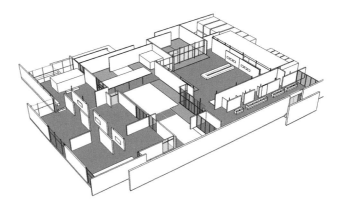

A temporary 8,200 sq. ft. building, with a disk architecture that interprets the CI guidelines of BMW, was constructed for the four-week BMW Dealer Drive Event in Valencia. Up to 85% of it consisted of reusable materials and building sections. Because of its geometry, it can be simultaneously employed for various functions such as product positioning and staging. The building is a model for future showrooms.

Für den vierwöchigen BMW Dealer Drive Event wurde in Valencia ein temporäres, 2500 m² großes Gebäude errichtet, dessen Scheibenarchitektur die architektonischen CI-Richtlinien von BMW interpretierte. Es bestand zu 85% aus wieder einsetzbaren Materialien und Bauteilen und konnte aufgrund seiner Geometrie zeitgleich in unterschiedlichen Funktionen, wie Produktpositionierung- und Inszenierung, genutzt werden. Das Gebäude ist Vorbild für zukünftige Showrooms.

Para las cuatro semanas de las Jornadas de Conducción para Distribuidores que BMW celebró en Valencia, se levantó una edificación efímera de 2.500 m² con una arquitectura de grandes cristaleras acorde con la imagen corporativa de BMW. Se componía de un 85% de materiales y elementos reutilizables y, gracias a su geometría, permitía varias funciones de forma simultánea, tales como el posicionamiento del producto o su puesta en escena. Esta construcción servirá de modelo a próximos espacios expositivos.

Un bâtiment temporaire de 2500 m² avec une architecture en forme de disque, reflétant l'identité visuelle de BMW, a été construit pour les quatre semaines du BMW Dealer Drive Events à Valence. Il comprenait 85% de matériaux et sections de bâtiments réutilisables. En raison de sa géométrie, il pouvait être employé simultanément pour plusieurs fonctions, notamment le positionnement et la mise en scène du produit. Le bâtiment est un modèle pour de futurs showrooms.

Per l'evento BMW Dealer Drive della durata di quattro settimane è stato costruito a Valencia un edificio temporaneo di 2500 m², che con un'architettura a vetrate ha interpretato le direttive architettoniche CI della BMW. Costituito al 85% da materiali ed elementi costruttivi riciclabili, è stato possibile utilizzarlo, in base alla sua geometria, allo stesso tempo in funzioni differenti come il posizionamento del prodotto e l'allestimento. L'edificio è un esempio per showroom futuri.

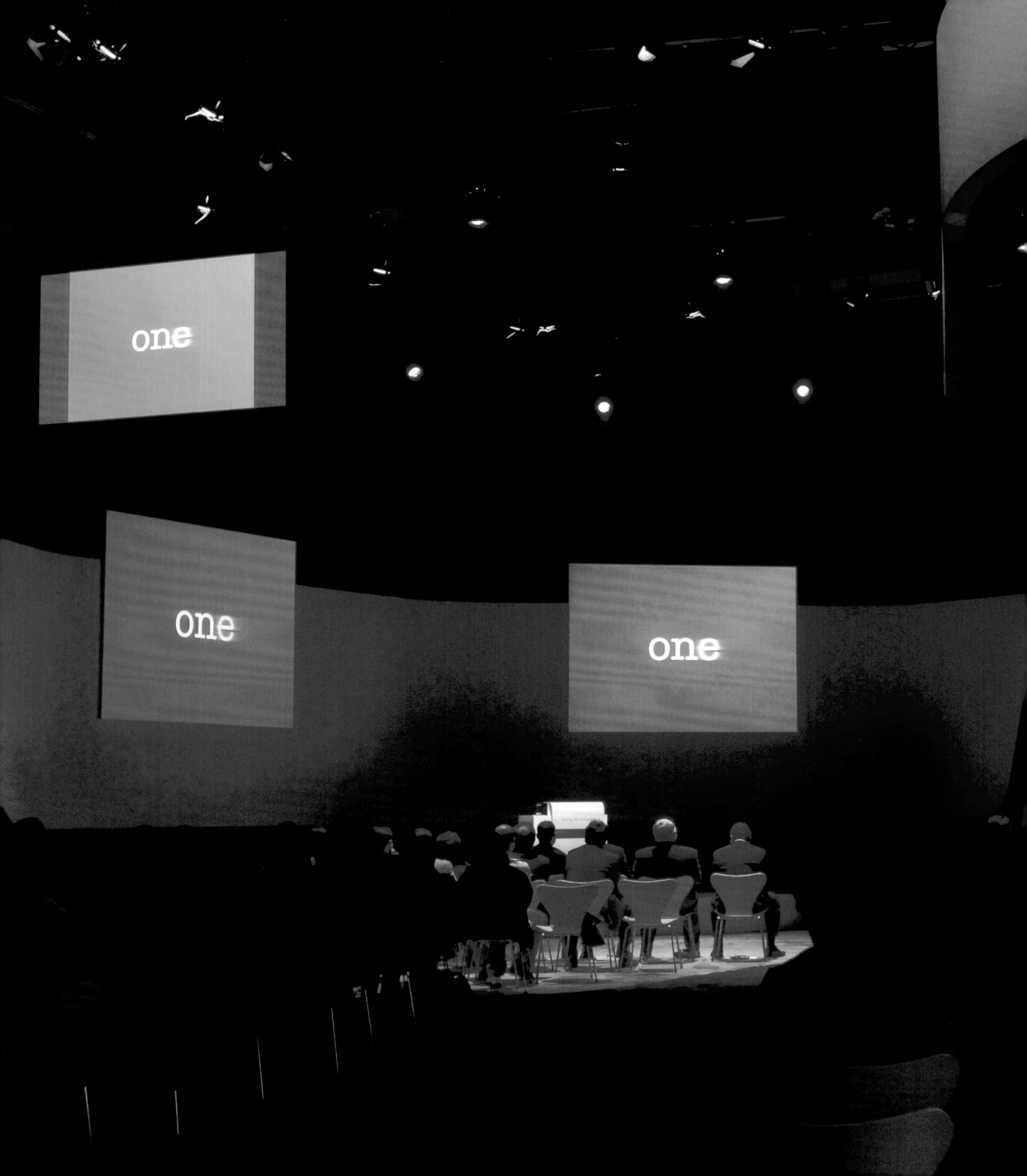
one
one
one

BLUE SCOPE COMMUNICATIONS | BERLIN
Sony Ericsson, Customer Event 2007
Athens, Greece | 1 March 2007
Photos: Katja Hoffmann for Blue Scope

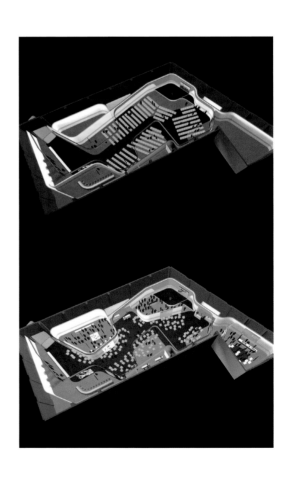

Sony Ericsson invited 250 major customers to a three-day event in Athens. The emphasis was a workshop in specially developed event architecture. After the plenary session, the guests rediscovered the space that had been converted during the lunch break: In three staged theme rooms, the protagonists conveyed the specific product features to the participants. Architecture and dramaturgy helped to better communicate the product lines.

Sony Ericsson lud 250 Großkunden zu einem dreitägigen Event nach Athen ein. Schwerpunkt war ein Workshop in eigens entwickelter Veranstaltungsarchitektur. Nach dem Plenum erlebten die Gäste den in der Mittagspause umgebauten Raum neu: In drei inszenierten Themenräumen vermittelten Akteure den Teilnehmern spezifische Produktfeatures. Architektur und Dramaturgie halfen die Produktlinien besser zu kommunizieren.

Sony Ericsson invitó a 250 grandes clientes a un evento en Atenas de tres días de duración. El acto central fue la celebración de un seminario en un espacio diseñado para la ocasión. Tras la sesión plenaria, la sala se transformó, y en los tres espacios temáticos resultantes, unos actores mostraron a los presentes las especificidades de los productos. Arquitectura y dramaturgia contribuyeron a una mejor asimilación de las líneas de productos.

Sony Ericsson a invité 250 grands clients à une manifestation de trois jours à Athènes. Le clou en était un atelier avec une architecture spécialement créée pour l'occasion. Après la session plénière, les invités ont redécouvert l'espace qui avait été transformé pendant la pause-déjeuner : dans trois pièces à thème, les protagonistes ont décrit les caractéristiques principales des produits aux participants. L'architecture et la dramaturgie permettaient de mieux communiquer sur les gammes de produit.

La Sony Ericsson ha invitato 250 compratori all'ingrosso a un evento della durata di tre giorni ad Atene. Il fulcro della manifestazione è stato il workshop in un'architettura sviluppata appositamente per la manifestazione. Dopo il plenum gli ospiti hanno vissuto una nuova sala che è stata trasformata durante la pausa pranzo: in tre aree tematiche inscenate degli attori hanno trasmesso ai partecipanti delle caratteristiche specifiche del prodotto. L'architettura e la drammaturgia hanno aiutato a comunicare meglio le linee del prodotto.

CIRC CORPORATE EXPERIENCE | WIESBADEN
BASF AG
pack.it 2006, La Reflexion du Fond
Ludwigshafen, Germany | 4 – 5 September 2006
Photos: Roger Richter

In 2006, the French artist Xavier Juillot covered the commercial building of BASF AG in Ludwigshafen with 13,124 sq. ft. of aluminum-coated polyamide fabric. The purpose was to demonstrate BASF's expertise in the packaging field to representatives of the packaging industry. Within the scope of the 2006 pack.it event, an interactive exhibition showed the guests how 35 new raw materials can be used for packaging.

Im Jahr 2006 verhüllte der französische Künstler Xavier Juillot das Gesellschaftshaus der BASF AG in Ludwigshafen mit 4000 m² aluminium-beschichtetem Polyamidgewebe, um Vertretern der Verpackungsindustrie die Expertise der BASF im Bereich Verpackungen zu zeigen. Im Rahmen der Veranstaltung pack.it 2006 offenbarte eine interaktive Ausstellung den Gästen die Einsatzfähigkeit von 35 neuen Grundstoffen für Verpackungen.

En el año 2006, el artista francés Xavier Juillot envolvió la central de BASF AG en Ludwigshafen (Alemania) en 4.000 m² de tejido de poliamida recubierto con una capa de aluminio con el objetivo de mostrar a los representantes de la industria del embalaje la experiencia que BASF tiene en este campo. En el marco de la "pack.it 2006", una exposición interactiva presentó a los asistentes las diferentes aplicaciones de 35 nuevos materiales de embalaje.

En 2006, l'artiste français Xavier Juillot a couvert le siège commercial de BASF AG à Ludwigshafen de 4000 m² de polyamide recouvert d'aluminium. Le but était de démontrer aux représentants de l'industrie du packaging l'expertise de BASF dans ce domaine. Dans le cadre de la manifestation pack.it de 2006, une exposition interactive montrait aux visiteurs comment 35 nouvelles matières premières pouvaient être utilisées dans l'emballage.

Nel 2006 l'artista francese Xavier Juillot ha impacchettato la sede della società BASF AG a Ludwigshafen con 4000 m² di tessuto in poliammide rivestito di alluminio, per mostrare ai rappresentanti dell'industria dell'imballaggio l'esperienza della BASF nel settore imballaggio. Nell'ambito della manifestazione pack.it 2006 una mostra interattiva ha rivelato agli ospiti la capacità di utilizzo di 35 nuove materie prime per imballaggi.

DESIGN COMPANY | MUNICH
Frank Walder, VIP trader's event
Dusseldorf, Germany | 2005
Photos: Michael Ingenweyen

As an alternative to presenting the new fashion brand Frank Walder with a collection, the Design Company relied on the visualized brand values at the initial events. A considerable component of the new positioning was the graphic concept with the company logo. It was also possible to experience the brand on the various interaction surfaces through live cooking, a reading with Corinna Harfouch, and music entertainment.

Anstatt die neue Modemarke Frank Walder mit einer Kollektion zu präsentieren, setzte die Design Company bei den ersten Events auf die visualisierten Markenwerte. Ein wesentlicher Bestandteil der Neu-Positionierung war das Grafikkonzept mit Firmenlogo. Auf verschiedenen Interaktionsflächen wurde die Marke zudem durch Live Cooking, eine Lesung mit Corinna Harfouch und Musik Entertainment erlebbar gemacht.

En lugar de presentar la nueva firma de moda Frank Walder con una colección, Design Company puso el énfasis en visualizar los valores de la marca en los primeros eventos. Un componente esencial de este nuevo posicionamiento fue el concepto gráfico del logotipo de la firma. En distintas superficies interactivas se pudo percibir lo que significa esta marca con cocina en directo, una charla de Corinna Harfouch y divertimentos musicales.

Plutôt que de présenter la nouvelle marque de mode Frank Walder avec une collection, Design Compagny s'est appuyé sur les valeurs de la marque visualisées lors d'événements précédents. Une composante majeure du nouveau positionnement était le concept graphique avec le logo de la compagnie. Il était également possible de faire l'expérience de la marque dans les diverses surfaces d'interaction à travers des démonstrations de cuisine, une lecture de Corinna Harfouch et de la musique.

Invece di presentare il nuovo marchio di moda Frank Walder tramite una collezione, la Design Company ha puntato, nell'ambito del primo evento, su valori del marchio visualizzati. Una parte importante del nuovo posizionamento è stato il concetto grafico con il logo della ditta. Su diverse superfici interattive il marchio è stato vissuto anche attraverso il Live Cooking, una lettura con Corinna Harfouch e con dell'intrattenimento musicale.

DESIGN COMPANY | MUNICH
Sony Germany GmbH
IFA 2005, Staging of product like.no.other.
Berlin, Germany | 2005
Photos: Michael Ingenweyen

At the 2005 IFA in Berlin, Sony Germany decided upon the visual depiction of the claim "like.no.other." Instead of a fair appearance in the customary sense, it was an experiential space of the Sony world: No stand personnel attended to the visitors. Instead, the guests moved through suspended lengths of material and discovered independent theme worlds of entertainment electronics.

Bei der IFA 2005 in Berlin entschied sich Sony Deutschland für die visuelle Darstellung des Claims „like.no.other". Es war kein Messeauftritt im herkömmlichen Sinn, sondern ein Erfahrungsraum der Sonywelt: Kein Standpersonal kümmerte sich um die Besucher, stattdessen bewegten sich die Gäste durch abgehängte Stoffbahnen und entdeckten selbstständig Themenwelten der Unterhaltungselektronik.

En la IFA 2005 de Berlín, Sony Alemania se decidió por representar visualmente el eslogan "like.no.other". No se trataba de la convencional presencia en una feria, sino de un espacio para experimentar el mundo de Sony. El stand carecía de personal para atender a los visitantes. En este caso, los invitados se movían por unas pasarelas suspendidas y descubrían por sí mismos los diferentes mundos de la electrónica de consumo.

Lors de l'IFA 2005 à Berlin, Sony Allemagne a choisi de dépeindre visuellement le slogan « like.no.other ». Plutôt qu'une participation à la foire au sens conventionnel, c'était un espace d'expérimentation du monde de Sony : aucun personnel n'attendait les visiteurs au stand, mais ils se déplaçaient à travers des hauteurs de matériel suspendu et découvraient des mondes indépendants sur le thème de l'électronique de loisirs.

In occasione della IFA 2005 a Berlino la Sony Deutschland si è decisa per una rappresentazione visuale dell'affermazione „like.no.other". Non è stata una presenza presso la fiera nel senso tradizionale del termine, ma un ambiente per fare esperienza nel mondo Sony: non c'era del personale allo stand a prendersi cura del visitatore, al contrario gli ospiti si sono mossi all'interno di pezzi di stoffa appesi e hanno scoperto autonomamente i mondi tematici dell'elettronica da intrattenimento.

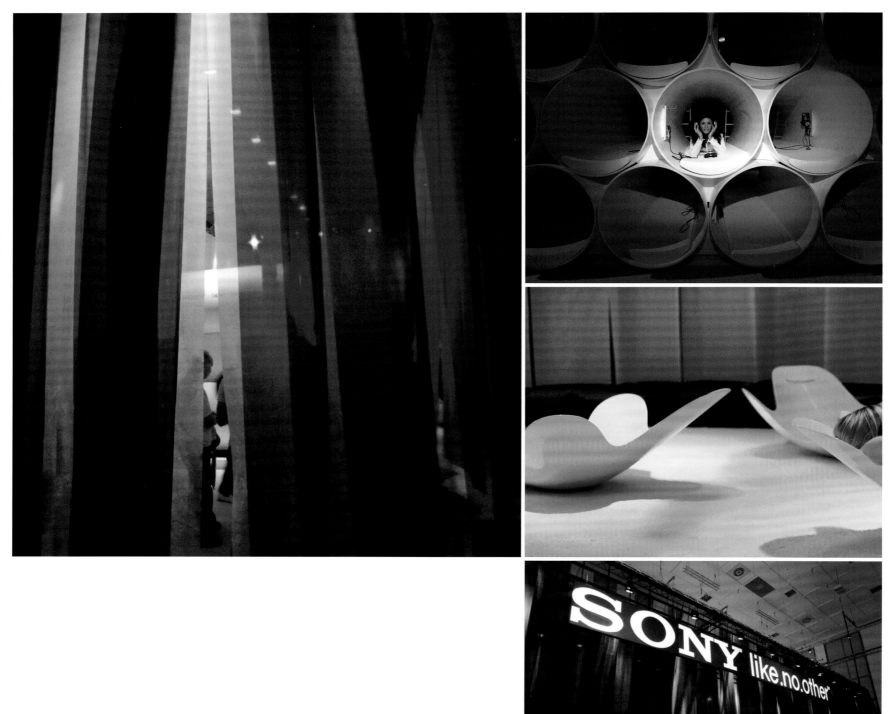

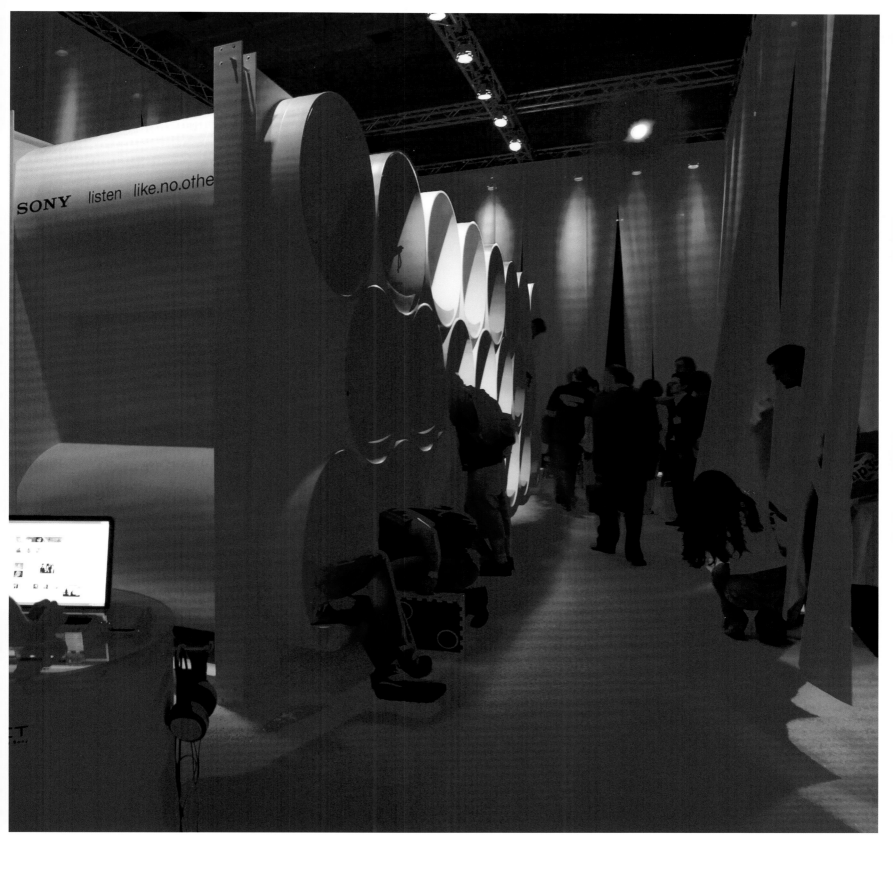

EVENTLABS | HAMBURG
Volkswagen AG, Project Fox
Copenhagen, Denmark | April 2005
Photos: diephotodesigner.de

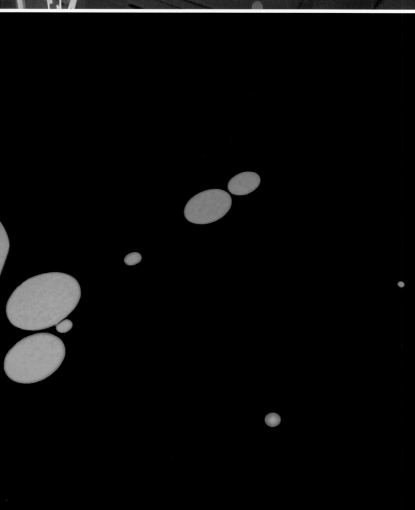

Project Fox was an unusual driving presentation intended to promote the image of the VW Fox as a young, modern city car. For this purpose, the Volkswagen AG invited representatives of the VW Fox target group—young cooks, artists, architects, and others—to Copenhagen so they could create unique destinations for young people according to their own ideas: for example, the Hotel and the Club Fox.

Das Projekt Fox war eine ungewöhnliche Fahrpräsentation, die dem Image des VW Fox als junges, modernes Stadtauto gerecht werden sollte. Die Volkswagen AG lud dafür Vertreter aus der Zielgruppe des VW Fox - junge Köche, Künstler, Architekten und andere - nach Kopenhagen ein, um einzigartige Destinationen für junge Menschen gemäß ihrer Vorstellung zu kreieren: zum Beispiel das Hotel und den Club Fox.

El Proyecto Fox fue una presentación poco convencional. Su objeto era promocionar la imagen del Volkswagen Fox como un coche urbano, moderno y juvenil. Para ello, la firma invitó a Copenhague a representantes del destinatario potencial del coche -jóvenes cocineros, arquitectos, etc.-, con el fin de crear destinos únicos para ellos basándose en sus propias ideas, como por ejemplo el Hotel y el Club Fox.

Le Projet Fox était une présentation originale conçue pour promouvoir l'image de la Fox VW en tant que voiture urbaine et jeune. Dans ce but, l'AG Volkswagen a invité des personnes représentatives du groupe cible VW Fox – jeunes cuisiniers, artistes, architectes, et autres – à Copenhague, où ils ont pu créer des destinations uniques pour les jeunes gens selon leurs idées : par exemple, l'Hôtel et le Club Fox.

Il Progetto Fox è stato una presentazione in movimento fuori dal comune, che ha voluto essere all'altezza della VW Fox in quanto macchina utilitaria giovane e moderna. La Volkswagen AG ha invitato per questa occasione alcuni rappresentanti dei destinatari della VW Fox - giovani cuochi, artisti, architetti e altri - a Copenaghen per creare delle destinazioni uniche per delle persone giovani in conformità con le loro idee: per esempio l'Hotel e il Club Fox.

EVENTLABS | HAMBURG
Marc Cain, Marc Cain Temporary Eventroom
Berlin, Germany | 2 February 2006
Photos: diephotodesigner.de

For an event during the CPD fashion fair in Dusseldorf, eventlabs completely redesigned the Marc Cain Showroom according to the collection motto. For the staging of "Noble White," they worked exclusively with white light and the color white—white floors, white walls, white chairs. All of the illuminated surfaces were projection surfaces that accompany the overall production.

Für eine Veranstaltung während der Modemesse CPD in Düsseldorf gestaltete eventlabs den Marc Cain Showroom gemäß dem Kollektionsmotto komplett um. Für die Inszenierung „Nobel White" wurde ausschließlich mit weißem Licht und der Farbe Weiß gearbeitet - weiße Böden, weiße Wände, weiße Stühle. Sämtliche erleuchteten Flächen sind Projektionsflächen, die die Gesamtinszenierung begleiteten.

eventlabs rediseñó de arriba abajo el showroom de Marc Cain para un desfile en el marco de la feria de moda CPD de Dusseldorf. Para escenificar "Nobel White" se utilizó exclusivamente luz blanca en un decorado completamente blanco: suelo, paredes y sillas blancas. La producción vino acompañada con proyecciones sobre las superficies iluminadas.

Pour une soirée pendant la fête de la mode CPD à Düsseldorf, eventlabs a redessiné le Showroom Marc Cain selon le leitmotiv de la collection. Pour la mise en scène de « Noble White », les designers ont travaillé uniquement avec de la lumière blanche et la couleur blanche – sols blancs, murs blancs, chaises blanches. Toutes les surfaces illuminées étaient des surfaces de projection qui accompagnaient la mise en scène générale.

Per una rappresentazione durante la fiera di moda CPD a Düsseldorf la eventlabs ha completamente riorganizzato lo showroom Marc Cain in conformità con il motto della collezione. Per l'allestimento „Nobel White" si è lavorato esclusivamente con luce bianca e colore bianco - pavimenti bianchi, pareti bianche, sedie bianche. Tutte le superfici illuminate sono superfici di proiezione che hanno accompagnato tutta la messa in scena.

EVENTLABS | HAMBURG
Marc Cain, Store Opening
Berlin, Germany | 5 October 2005
Photos: diephotodesigner.de

Since 2005, eventlabs has been in charge of Marc Cain at his brand appearances and stages all of the store openings throughout Germany within this context. In this process, the focus is on the visual interpretation of the respective collection theme—achieved here through floral patterns projected on the wall. At the same time, the intent is to emphasize the spacious and unusual brand architecture of the stores.

Seit 2005 betreut eventlabs Marc Cain bei seinen Markenauftritten und inszeniert in diesem Zusammenhang deutschlandweit alle Store-Eröffnungen. Der Focus liegt dabei auf der visuellen Umsetzung des jeweiligen Kollektionsthemas, hier erreicht durch an die Wand projizierte florale Muster. Gleichzeitig soll die großzügige und außergewöhnliche Markenarchitektur der Stores betont werden.

eventlabs se encarga desde 2005 de la presencia en el mercado de Marc Cain. Por ello corre a cargo de todas las inauguraciones de sus tiendas en Alemania. En ellas, el foco de atención es la interpretación visual de los temas de cada colección, que aquí se consigue proyectando en la pared motivos florales. Asimismo, se intenta remarcar la amplitud y la insólita arquitectura de sus establecimientos.

Depuis 2005, eventlabs est en charge de Marc Cain pour les apparitions de la marque et met en scène toutes les ouvertures de magasin à travers l'Allemagne. Dans ce cadre, la focalisation est faite sur l'interprétation des différents thèmes de la collection, réussie ici grâce à des motifs floraux projetés sur le mur. Dans le même temps, l'intention est de mettre l'emphase sur l'architecture spacieuse et originale des magasins.

Dal 2005 la eventlabs segue Marc Cain durante le presentazioni del suo marchio e mette in scena, in questo contesto, tutte le aperture degli store a livello nazionale in Germania. Il punto focale si trova in questo caso nella trasformazione visuale del relativo tema della collezione, qui raggiunta tramite motivi floreali proiettati alla parete. Al contempo si vuole sottolineare l'architettura di marca generosa e straordinaria dello store.

EVENTLABS | HAMBURG
Volkswagen AG
VW IROC Concept car media presentation
Berlin, Germany | 24 August 2006
Photos: diephotodesigner.de

Volkswagen presented the concept study IROC on a speedway circling the audience in the Berlin Tempelhof airport on 33,000 sq. ft. Using video projections and a transparent LED, the vehicle became part of a spectacular media production: The viewer could hardly distinguish between the real events and the video image. The car only assumed its true form on the stage.

Auf 10.000 m² präsentierte Volkswagen im Berliner Flughafen Tempelhof die Konzeptstudie IROC auf einem um das Publikum laufenden Speedway. Anhand von Videoprojektionen und einer transparenten LED wurde das Fahrzeug Teil einer spektakulären Medieninszenierung – der Betrachter konnte zwischen realem und Video-Bild nicht mehr unterscheiden. Erst auf der Bühne nahm der Wagen wirklich Gestalt an.

Volkswagen presentó en una superficie de 10.000 m² su prototipo IROC en un circuito que rodeaba a los presentes en el aeropuerto berlinés de Tempelhof. Mediante videoproyecciones y luminosos transparentes, el vehículo participó en una espectacular producción audiovisual. A la audiencia le costaba distinguir entre imagen real y proyectada. Fue ya en el escenario donde el automóvil tomó cuerpo.

Volkswagen a présenté le concept IROC sur une voie rapide entourant le public à l'aéroport Tempelhof de Berlin sur 10 000 m². Grâce à des projections vidéo et un écran DEL transparent, le véhicule faisait partie d'une production média extraordinaire : le spectateur pouvait difficilement distinguer le réel de l'image vidéo. C'est seulement sur la scène que la voiture a repris sa forme réelle.

In un'area di 10.000 m² la Volkswagen ha presentato nell'aeroporto di Berlino Tempelhof lo studio concettuale IROC su una pista che girava intorno al pubblico. Tramite videoproiettori e un LED trasparente il veicolo è divenuto parte di un allestimento mediatico spettacolare: l'osservatore non era più in grado di distinguere tra l'immagine reale e quella video. Solo sul palcoscenico la macchina a preso forma reale.

FACTS+FICTION | COLOGNE
ING-DiBa, Icehouse
Various locations, Germany
18 December 2005 - 7 February 2006
Photos: facts+fiction

In six large German cities, the German direct banking service ING-DiBa had an unusual ice house built in a loft style so that it could leave the anonymity of the internet and be experienced by the public. Almost 1,000 blocks of ice weighing 320 pounds each were produced in advance and then shaped. The bank wanted to illustrate its transparent values and openness to the customers by using the ice.

In sechs deutschen Großstädten ließ die deutsche Direktbank ING-DiBa ein außergewöhnliches Eishaus im Loft-Stil errichten, um aus der Anonymität des Internets herauszutreten und sich öffentlich erlebbar zu machen. Dafür wurden knapp 1000 Eisblöcke à 145 kg vorproduziert und dann bearbeitet. Durch das Eis wollte die Bank ihre transparenten Werte und ihre Offenheit gegenüber den Kunden verdeutlichen.

En seis populosas ciudades alemanas erigió la germana de banca directa ING-DiBa una insólita casa de hielo a modo de loft. Así abandonaba el anonimato de Internet y se presentaba al público. Para ello hizo falta elaborar y tallar casi 1.000 bloques de hielo de 145 kg cada uno. El banco quiso transmitir con el hielo la transparencia de sus valores y el contacto directo con el cliente.

Dans six grandes villes allemandes, le service de banque directe ING-DiBa avait fait construire une maison de glace originale dans le style loft, pour dépasser le côté anonyme d'internet et permettre au public de vivre une expérience. Près de 1000 blocs de glace de 145 kg chacun on été préparés à l'avance puis taillés. En utilisant la glace, la banque voulait illustrer ses valeurs de transparence et d'ouverture vers les clients.

La banca diretta ING-DiBa ha fatto costruire in sei grandi città tedesche una casa di ghiaccio fuori dal comune in stile loft per uscire dall'anonimato di Internet e per poter essere vissuta pubblicamente. Per fare questo sono stati anticipatamente prodotti quasi 1000 blocchi di ghiaccio da 145 kg, successivamente lavorati. Tramite il ghiaccio la banca ha voluto chiarire i suoi valori trasparenti e la sua apertura verso i clienti.

FACTS+FICTION | COLOGNE
Nissan, European Dealer Convention
Barcelona, Spain | 23 November 2004
Photos: Jörg Küster

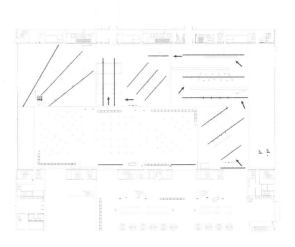

143

In order to present the reorientation of the brand to its dealers, Nissan chose an exhibition that involved the guests. After a brief introduction, an audio guide took them through the individual rooms in the new convention center of Barcelona to explore the significance of a strong brand in a competitive environment.

Um seinen Händlern die gestraffte Produktpalette und eine Neuorientierung in Richtung Lifestyle zu präsentieren, wählte Nissan eine die Gäste involvierende Ausstellung. Nach einer kurzen Einführung ging es im neuen Kongresszentrum in Barcelona mit Audio-Guides durch die einzelnen Räume, die die Bedeutung einer starken Marke in einem wettbewerbsintensiven Umfeld thematisierten.

En seis populosas ciudades alemanas erigió la germana de banca directa ING-DiBa una insólita casa de hielo a modo de loft. Así abandonaba el anonimato de Internet y se presentaba al público. Para ello hizo falta elaborar y tallar casi 1.000 bloques de hielo de 145 kg cada uno. El banco quiso transmitir con el hielo la transparencia de sus valores y el contacto directo con el cliente.

Afin de présenter la réorientation de la marque à ses vendeurs, Nissan a choisi une exposition qui impliquait les visiteurs. Après une brève introduction, un guide audio les emmenait à travers les diverses pièces dans le nouveau centre de convention de Barcelone pour envisager toute la signification de marque forte dans un environnement concurrentiel.

Per presentare ai suoi venditori il nuovo orientamento del suo marchio la Nissan ha presentato una mostra che ha coinvolto gli ospiti. Dopo una breve introduzione sono stati portati con audioguide nel nuovo centro congressi a Barcellona attraverso singoli ambienti. Ambienti che hanno rappresentato il significato di un marchio forte all'interno di un ambiente pieno di concorrenza.

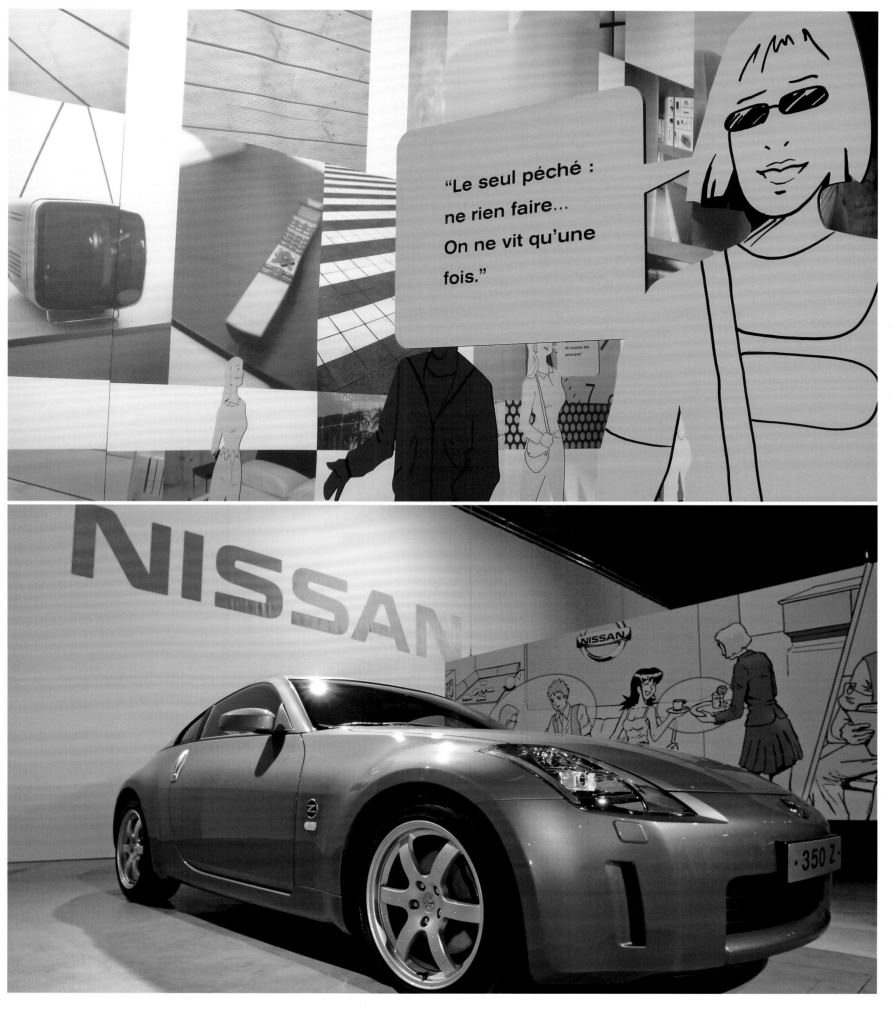

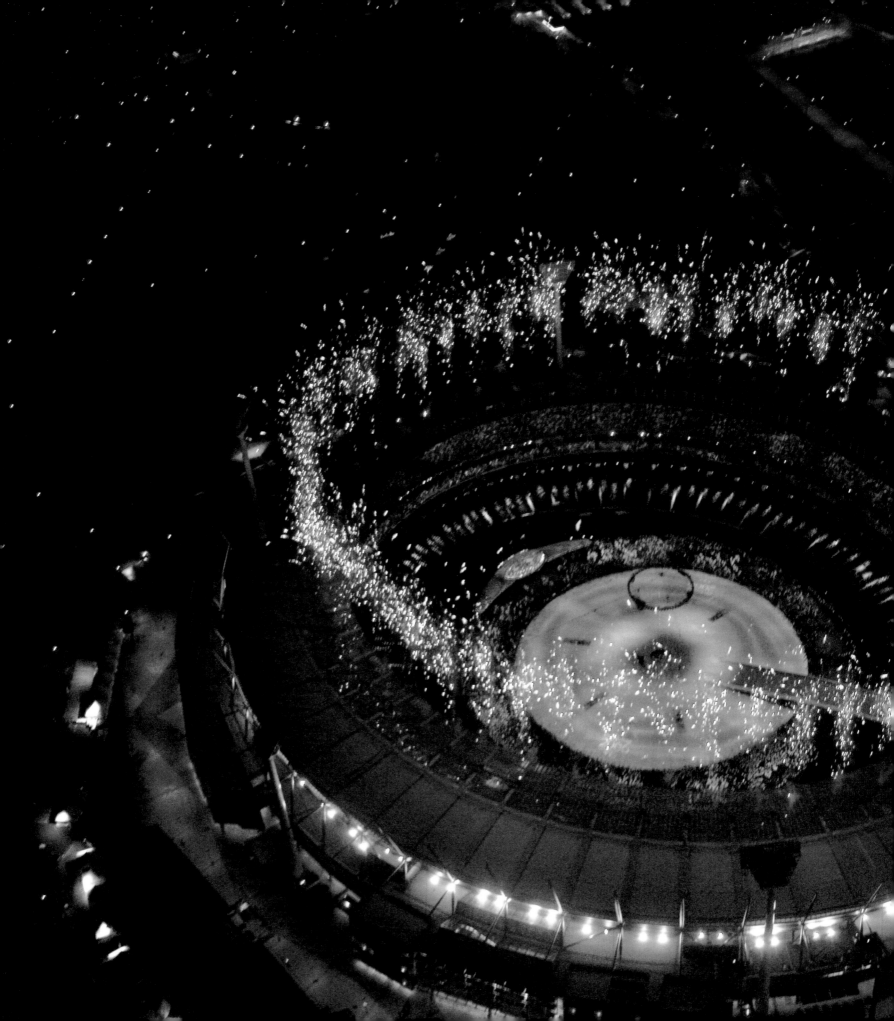

JACK MORTON | WORLDWIDE
Melbourne 2006 Commonwealth Games
Opening and Closing Ceremonies
Melbourne, Australia | 15 March and 26 March 2006
Photos: Getty Images

Melbourne was guaranteed worldwide attention for the opening and closing celebration of the 2006 Commonwealth Games. Event elements included a flying "tram," musical performances, varied performers and dancers. By taking the bold step of staging the ceremonies not only inside the Cricket Ground Stadium but also in the city's streets and river, the events inspired 1.4 billion television viewers and a live audience.

Weltweite Aufmerksamkeit war Melbourne mit der spektakulären Inszenierung von Eröffnungs- und Abschlussfeier der Commonwealth Games im Jahr 2006 garantiert. Zu den Shows gehörten eine „fliegende" Tram, Musikvorführungen, unterschiedliche Künstler und Tänzer. Durch den mutigen Schritt, die Feier nicht nur innerhalb des Cricket Ground Stadion zu halten, sondern auch in die Strassen der Stadt und an den Fluss zu gehen, inspirierten diese Veranstaltungen 1.4 Milliarden Fernsehzuschauer und ein Live-Publikum.

Melbourne tenía garantizada la atención mundial con las ceremonias de apertura y clausura de los Juegos de la Commonwealth de 2006. El espectáculo contó con un tranvía "volante", actuaciones musicales y conciertos. La arriesgada decisión de celebrar las ceremonias no solo en el interior del estadio, sino también en las calles y la ribera del río tuvo como resultado 1.400 millones de televidentes y una gran cantidad de público.

Melbourne était sûre d'attirer l'attention mondiale pour les cérémonies d'ouverture et de clôture des Jeux du Commonwealth 2006. Les manifestations comprenaient un tram « volant », des concerts, divers artistes et danseurs. Un pas a été franchi avec la mise en scène des cérémonies non seulement à l'intérieur du Cricket Ground Stadium mais aussi dans les rues et sur la rivière de la ville, les manifestations ont ainsi inspiré 1,4 milliards de téléspectateurs et un large public sur place.

Melbourne si è garantita l'attenzione del mondo intero grazie all'apertura e alla chiusura delle celebrazioni per i Giochi del Commonwealth del 2006. Negli elementi dell'evento erano inclusi anche un "tram" volante, delle rappresentazioni musicalie, vari attori e ballerini. Nel prendere la decisione coraggiosa di portare la rappresentazione delle cerimonie non solo nel Cricket Ground Stadium ma anche sul fiume e nelle strade della città, gli eventi hanno fatto sognare 1,4 bilioni di spettatori davanti alle televisioni ed un pubblico dal vivo.

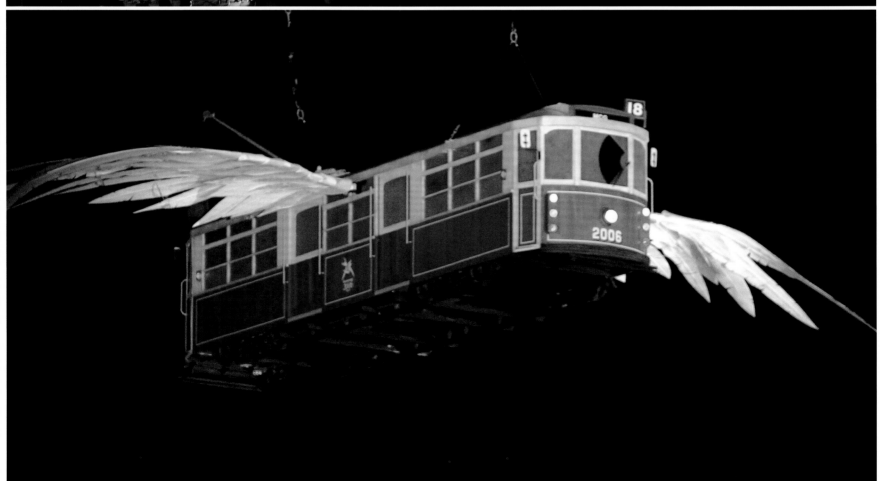

KMS TEAM GMBH | MUNICH
Daniela Müller
Private birthday party
Stuttgart, Germany | 16 September 2006
Photos: Daniel Grund, Florian Hagena, KMS

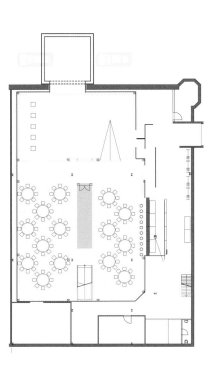

To celebrate a round-number birthday, Daniela Müller invited friends and acquaintances into her very own personal world. A black cube that exuded a festive aura through the brilliant purple—Daniela Müller's favorite color—on the inside and a white, peaceful room formed the "gateway" to the world of the hostess. The actual banquet hall had atmospheric elements and personal photos projected onto the transparent sheets.

Zu ihrem runden Geburtstag lud Daniela Müller Freunde und Bekannte in ihre ganz persönliche Welt ein. Ein schwarzer Kubus, der im Inneren durch leuchtendes Purpur – Daniela Müllers Lieblingsfarbe – eine feierliche Aura verströmte, und ein weißer ruhiger Raum bildeten das „Tor" zur Welt der Gastgeberin. Im eigentlichen Festsaal wurden stimmungsvolle Elemente und persönliche Fotos auf transparente Tücher projiziert.

Para celebrar el cumplimiento de un número redondo de años, Daniela Müller invitó a amigos y conocidos a su universo personal. Un cubo negro de cuyo interior irradiaba una alegre luz púrpura –el color preferido de Daniela Müller– y un sosegado espacio en blanco conformaban la "entrada" al universo de la anfitriona. En el salón se proyectaron sobre lienzos transparentes elementos emotivos y fotos personales.

Pour célébrer un anniversaire à chiffre rond, Daniela Müller a invité ses amis et connaissances dans son monde très personnel. Un cube noir qui exhalait une aura festive grâce un violet brillant – la couleur préférée de Daniela Müller – à l'intérieur et une pièce blanche et calme formaient une « entrée » vers le monde de l'hôtesse. La véritable salle de banquet contenait des éléments atmosphériques et des photos personnelles projetées sur des feuilles transparentes.

In occasione di un compleanno speciale Daniela Müller ha invitato amici e conoscenti ad entrare a far parte di un mondo del tutto personale. Un cubo nero, che al suo interno irradiava un' aurea festosa tramite un color porpora luminoso – il colore preferito di Daniela Müller – e una sala bianca e tranquilla hanno costituito la „porta" per il mondo della padrona di casa. Nel vero e proprio salone delle feste sono stati proiettati su dei teli trasparenti degli elementi suggestivi e delle foto personali.

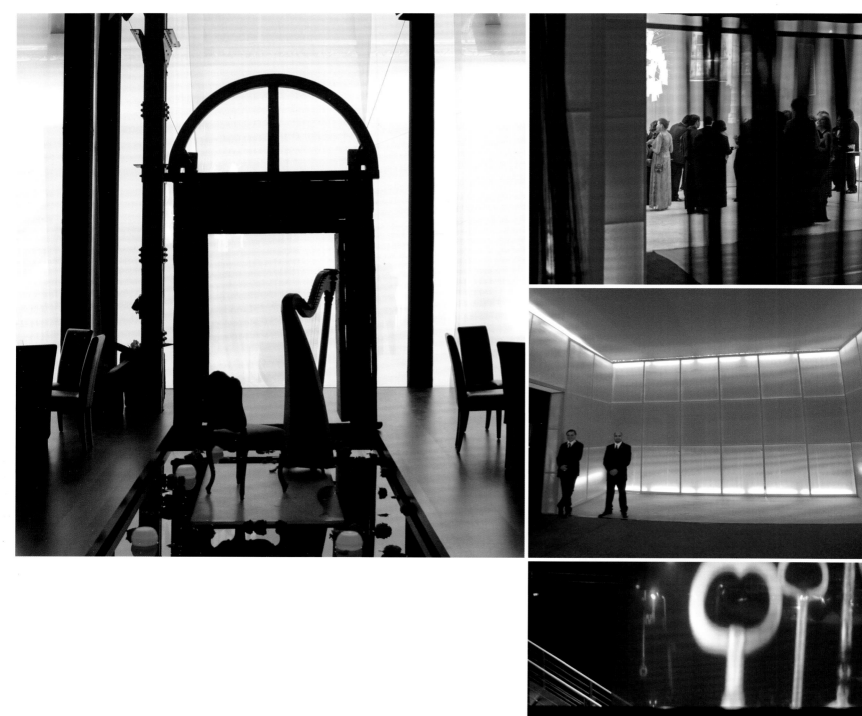

LIGANOVA | STUTTGART
Mercedes-Benz Motorsport
Show presentation CL- & GL-Klasse
Hockenheim, Germany | 2006
Photos: Liganova

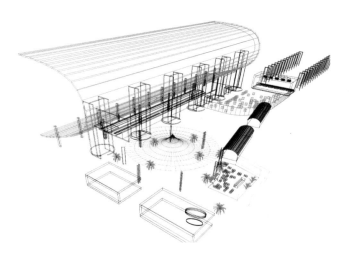

Mercedes Benz presented the new GL and CL class under the Mercedes stand in the Formula 1 racetrack of Hockenheim with the "Night of the Stars" event. Light installations, individually built lounges, and a 197-foot wide stage turned the 26,247 sq. ft. area into a brand-oriented arena. A car, fashion, and lifestyle show successfully staged the new models here.

Unter der Mercedes-Tribüne im Formel-1-Rennzirkel von Hockenheim stellte Mercedes Benz mit dem Event „Night of the Stars" die neue GL- und CL-Klasse vor. Lichtinstallationen, individuell gebaute Lounges und eine 60 Meter breite Bühne machten die 8000 m² große Fläche zur markengerechten Arena, in der eine Auto-, Mode- und Lifestyleshow die neuen Modelle gelungen in Szene setzte.

Mercedes Benz presentó con el espectáculo "La noche de las estrellas" sus nuevas clases GL y CL en su tribuna del circuito de fórmula 1 de Hockenheim. Los 8.000 m² con instalaciones de luz, lounges individuales y un escenario de 60 metros de anchura compusieron un marco a la altura de la marca. Fue un éxito la presentación de los modelos en un espectáculo con coches, moda y mucho estilo.

Mercedez-Benz a présenté les nouvelles classes GL et CL sous le stand Mercedes du circuit de Formule 1 d'Hockenheim pendant la « Nuit des Etoiles ». Des installations lumineuses, des stands construits individuellement et une scène de 60 mètres de long transformaient la zone de 8000 m² en une arène consacrée à la marque. Un show consacré à l'automobile, à la mode et au style de vie a présenté avec succès les nouveaux modèles.

Sotto la tribuna della Mercedes nel tracciato di Formula 1 di Hockenheim la Mercedes Benz ha presentato le nuove classi GL e CL con l'evento „Night of the Stars". Le installazioni delle luci, le lounges costruite individualmente e un palcoscenico largo 60 metri hanno trasformato la superficie di 8000 m² in una arena all'altezza del marchio, che ha visto protagonisti riusciti i nuovi modelli all'interno dello spettacolo di auto, di moda e dello stile di vita.

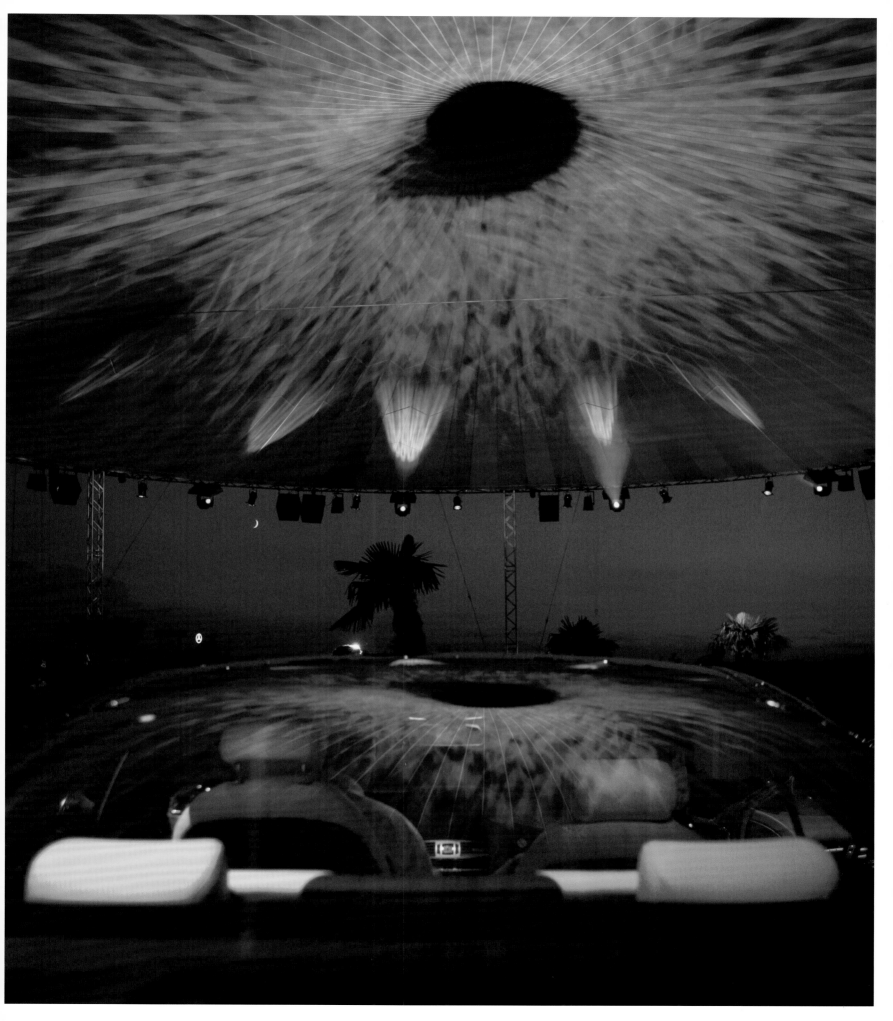

LIGANOVA | STUTTGART
Engelhorn, Presentation of collection 2006
Mannheim, Germany | 2006
Photos: Liganova

An old transformer factory, with its industrial character integrated into the concept, served as the location for the Engelhorn Fashion Show. In addition to the collection presentation on the catwalk, the fashion show consisted of trapeze, bodyart, and percussion artists. When a gigantic curtain fell at the end of the show, it revealed the lounge.

Als Location für die Engelhorn Fashion-Show diente ein altes Trafo-Werk, dessen industrieller Charakter in das visuelle Konzept der Veranstaltung integriert wurde. Die Fashion-Show selbst bestand neben der Kollektionspräsentation auf dem Laufsteg aus Luftakrobaten, Bodyart-Künstlern und Percussion-Künstlern. Der Fall eines riesigen Vorhangs am Ende der Show enthüllte schließlich die Lounge.

Una antigua planta transformadora fue elegida para el desfile de moda de Engelhorn. Su carácter industrial se integró en el concepto. Además de la presentación de la colección, por la pasarela también aparecieron trapecistas, practicantes del body-art y percusionistas. El lounge se descubrió al final del espectáculo tras la caída de un gigantesco telón.

Une ancienne usine de transformateurs, dont le caractère industriel était intégré au concept, a servi de décor au défilé de mode Engelhorn. Outre la présentation de la collection sur la passerelle, le défilé a également consisté en des performances de trapèze, de body art, et d'artistes percussionnistes. A la fin du spectacle, un immense rideau tomba, révélant le salon.

La location per il Fashion Show di Engelhorn è stata una vecchia fabbrica di trasformatori, che ha visto integrare il suo carattere industriale nel concetto. Il Fashion Show era costituito oltre alla presentazione della collezione sulla passerella anche da acrobati aerei, artisti di bodyart e di percussioni. La calata di un enorme sipario alla fine dello spettacolo ha infine rivelato la lounge.

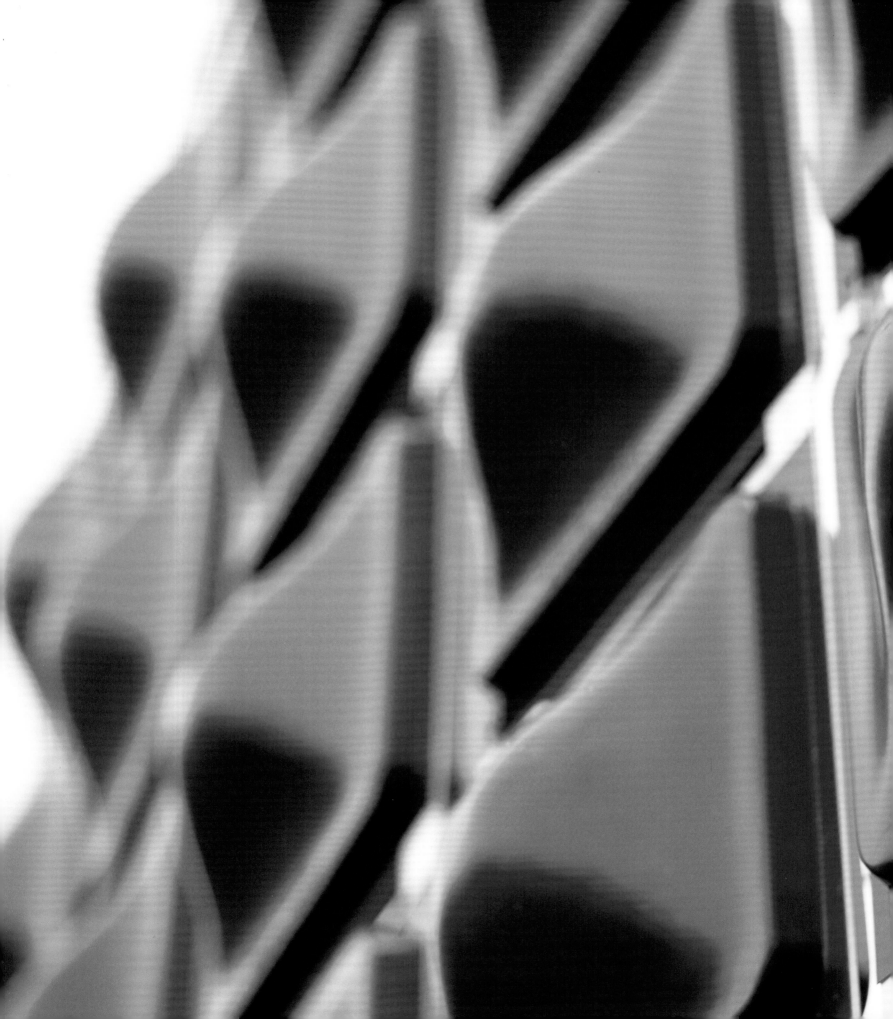

LIGHTLIFE | COLOGNE
City Nuremberg, Blue Night, Long night of museums
Nuremberg, Germany | 2003
Photos: Frank Rümmele

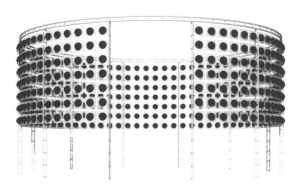

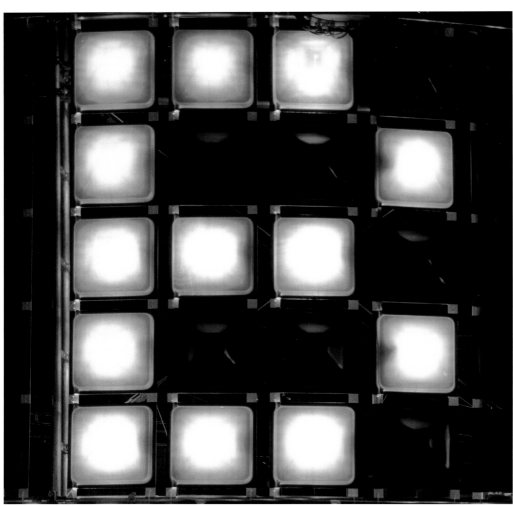

These three aluminum constructions with an individual height of 16,5 feet fascinated people at the Nuremberg Hauptmarkt during the "Blue Night of Nuremberg." The 400 controllable "pixels" of each construction showed texts and graphics, which had been set up in advance per internet. In addition, individual letters were depicted with pixels in front of the 22 museums. In the correct order, they resulted in the text "Blue Night—Line 2003."

Bei der „Blauen Nacht Nürnberg" faszinierten diese drei fünf Meter hohen Aluminiumkonstruktionen auf dem Nürnberger Hauptmarkt. Die je 400 steuerbaren „Pixel" zeigten Texte und Grafiken, die im Vorfeld per Internet eingereicht worden waren. Zudem wurden vor den 22 Museen mit Pixeln einzelne Buchstaben dargestellt, die in der richtigen Reihenfolge den Text „Blaue Nacht – Linie 2003" ergaben.

Estas tres construcciones de aluminio de cinco metros de altura cada una instaladas en el Hauptmarkt, causaron sensación durante la "Noche azul de Núremberg". Los 400 "píxeles" definibles de cada una de ellas mostraron mensajes y gráficos que previamente se configuraron en Internet. Asimismo, se colocaron letras ante los 22 museos que, leídas en el orden correcto, daban el siguiente mensaje: "Noche azul – Línea 2003".

Ces trois constructions en aluminium d'une hauteur de cinq mètres ont fasciné le public du Hauptmarkt de Nuremberg pendant la « Nuit bleue de Nuremberg ». Les 400 « pixels » contrôlables de chaque construction affichaient des textes et des graphiques, choisis à l'avance sur internet. En outre, diverses lettres étaient composées de pixels en face des 22 musées. Dans le bon ordre, elles formaient le texte « Nuit Bleue – Ligne 2003 ».

In occasione della „Notte Blu di Norimberga" hanno affascinato queste tre costruzioni in alluminio alte 5 metri e posizionate sul Hauptmarkt di Norimberga. Ognuno dei 400 „Pixel" pilotabili ha mostrato testi e grafici che erano stati inoltrati alla vigilia dell'evento tramite Internet. Inoltre sono state rappresentate singole lettere con Pixel davanti ai 22 musei, che nella giusta sequenza hanno rivelato il testo „Notte Blu – Linea 2003".

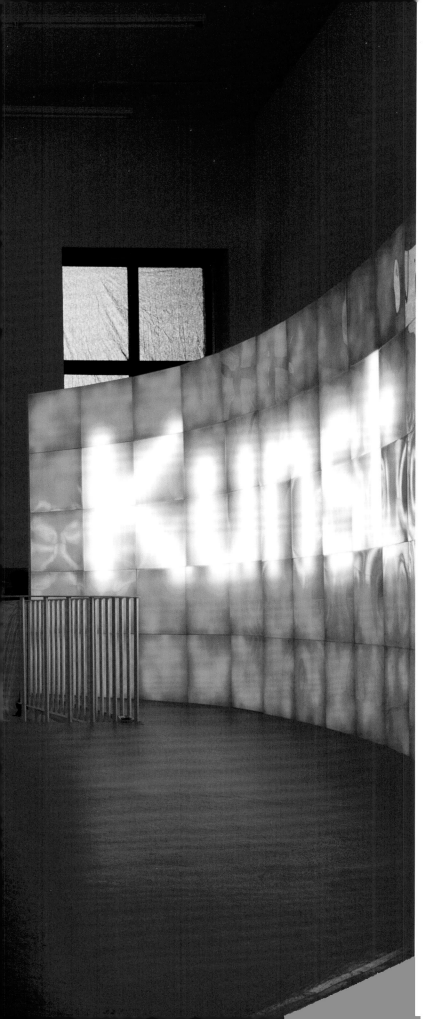

LIGHTLIFE | COLOGNE
Traxon Deutschland GmbH, Digital Moves
Frankfurt, Germany | 1 March 2006
Photos: Frank Rümmele

LightLife presented its Digital Moves installation—which was entered through a tunnel—at the 2006 Luminale. The image of the room was dominated by two large curved walls, equipped with LED tiles. Using microwave sensors, the number of visitors was scanned and evaluated: the more people entering the installation, the more exciting the light and color garment of the space.

Auf der Luminale 2006 stellte LightLife seine Installation „Digital Moves" vor, die man durch einen Tunnel betrat. Das Raumbild dominierten zwei große gebogene Wände, bestückt mit LED-Kacheln. Anhand von Mikrowellensensoren wurde die Anzahl der Besucher abgetastet und ausgewertet: Je mehr Menschen die Installation betraten, desto ereignisreicher wurden die Licht- und Farbkleider des Raums.

LightLife presentó su instalación "Digital Moves" (movimientos digitales) en la Luminale 2006. A la instalación se llegaba atravesando un túnel. El espacio estaba dominado por dos grandes paredes curvas compuestas por "azulejos de luz". Unos sensores de microondas escaneaban y contabilizaban el número de visitantes. A mayor número de personas, más llamativas eran las luces y los colores de la sala.

LightLife a présenté son installation « Digital Moves » – à laquelle on accédait par un tunnel – à l'édition 2006 de Luminale. L'image de la pièce était dominée par deux grands murs courbes, équipés de tuiles DEL. Grâce à des capteurs micro-ondes, le nombre des visiteurs était balayé et évalué : plus il y avait de personnes entrant dans l'installation, plus la lumière et la couleur de l'espace devenaient excitantes.

Alla Luminale 2006 la LightLife ha presentato la sua installazione „Digital Moves" alla quale si accedeva tramite un tunnel. L'immagine d'insieme dell'ambiente era dominato da due grandi pareti curve che erano rivestite da mattonelle LED. Tramite sensori a microonde è stata analizzata e valutata la quantità dei visitatori: più persone entravano nell'installazione, più ricchi di eventi diventavano i rivestimenti di luci e colori dell'ambiente.

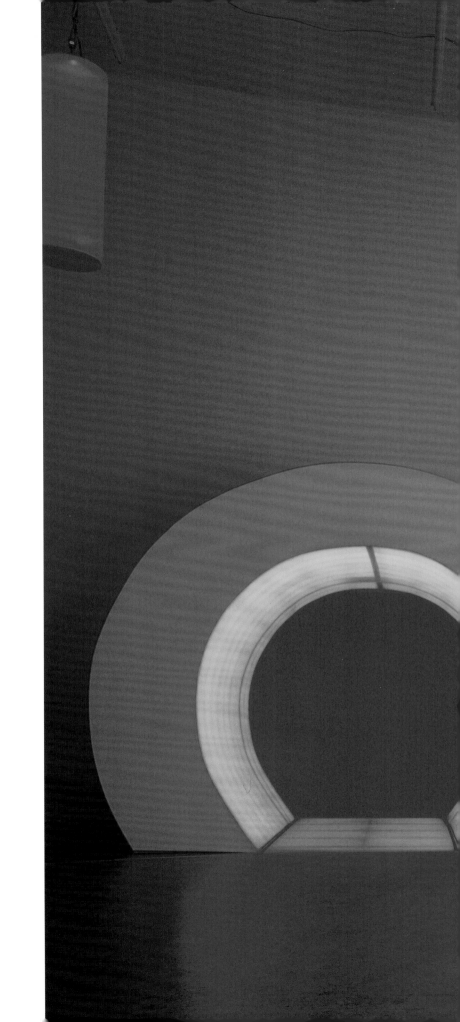

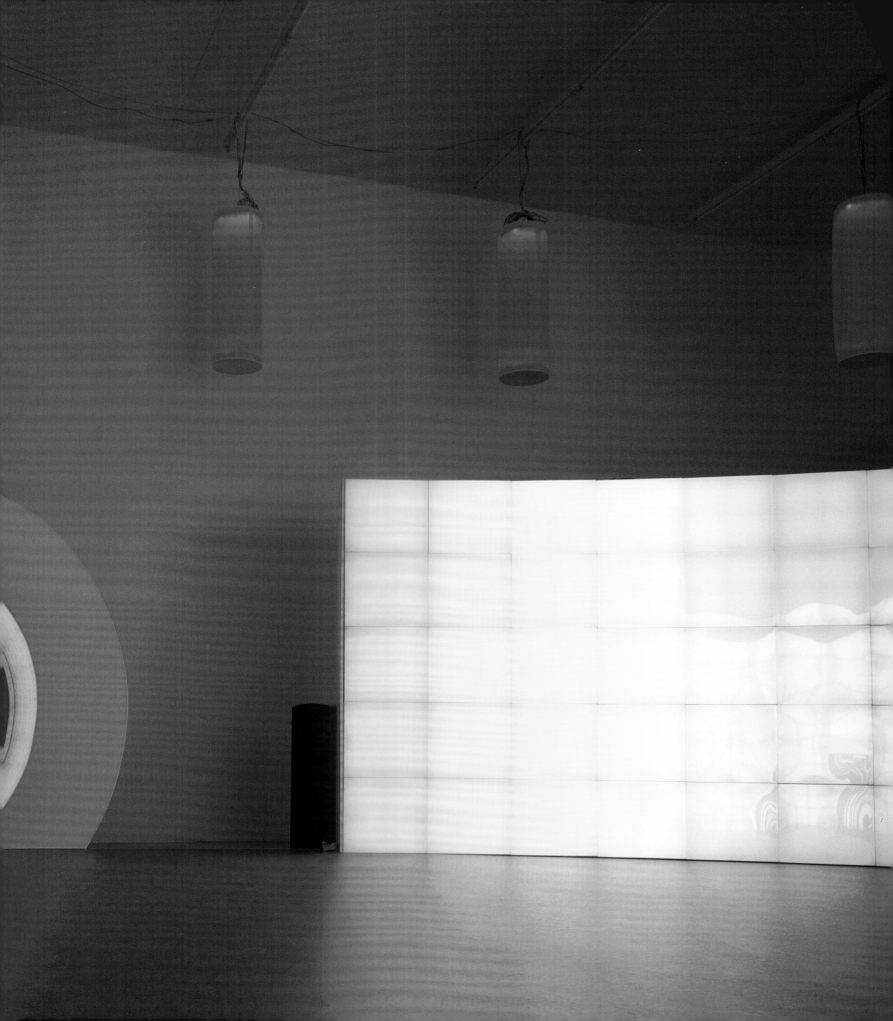

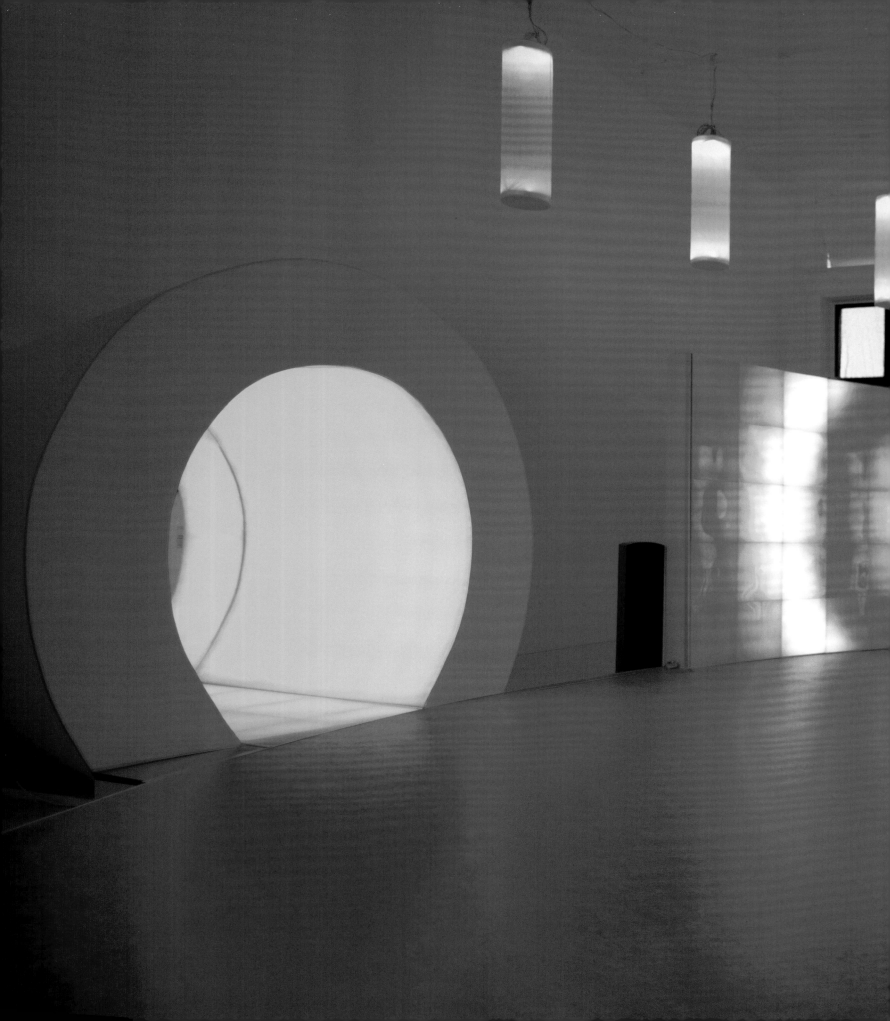

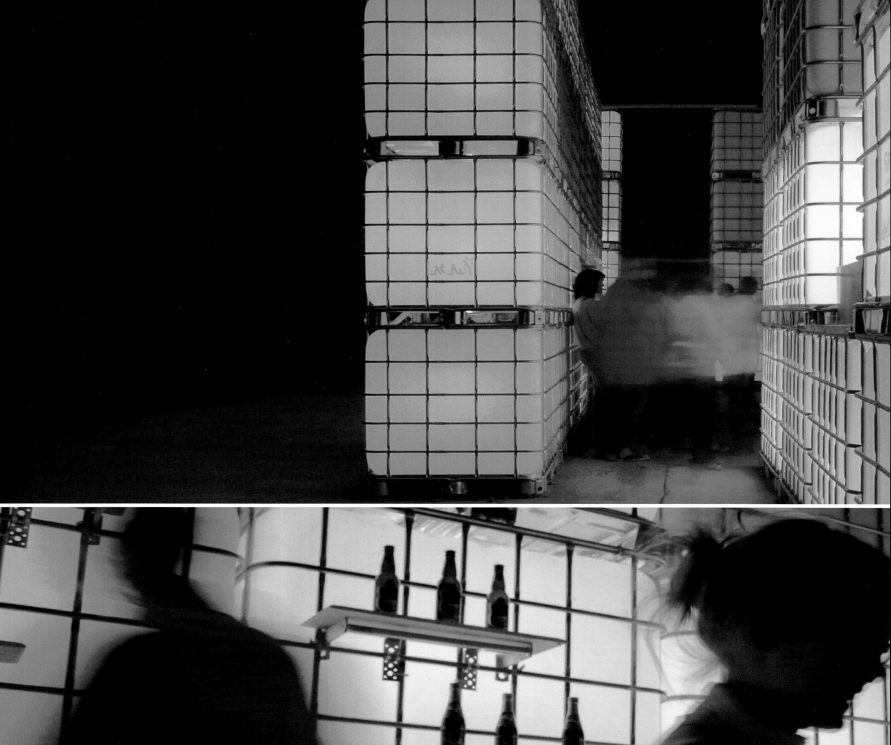

LIGHTLIFE | COLOGNE
Balestra Berlin, Kubik
Barcelona, Berlin, Lisbon | 2006/2007
Photos: Robert Ostmann (Berlin), Johannes Hubrich (Lisbon),
Robin Thomas (Barcelona)

After the success of "Kubik" in Berlin, the illuminated cubes simultaneously attracted a large audience in Barcelona and Lisbon. 270 conventional 1,000-quart water tanks were equipped with luminous devices for this purpose and could already be seen from far away as a result. Through individually controllable lamps, the various VJs were able to "program" the tanks of the open-air club and then play them in a visual way.

Nach dem Erfolg von „Kubik" in Berlin zogen die illuminierten Würfel zeitgleich in Barcelona und Lissabon ein großes Publikum an. 270 herkömmliche 1000-Liter-Wassertanks waren dafür mit Leuchtmitteln versehen worden und so schon von weitem zu erkennen. Durch einzeln steuerbare Lampen konnten verschiedene VJs die Tanks des Open-Air-Clubs „programmieren" und damit visuell bespielen.

Después del éxito del "Kubik" de Berlín, los dados iluminados atrajeron a un gran público de forma simultánea en Barcelona y Lisboa. 270 tanques de agua convencionales de 1.000 litros de capacidad estaban equipados con sistemas de iluminación con los que se les distinguía desde la distancia. Los VJs "programaban" uno a uno los focos dirigidos a los tanques de este club al aire libre, creando un espectáculo visual.

Après le succès de « Kubik » à Berlin, les cubes illuminés ont attiré un large public à Barcelone et à Lisbonne. 270 réservoirs d'eau de 1000 litres ont été équipés d'appareils lumineux dans ce but et pouvaient donc être vus de très loin. A l'aide de lampes contrôlables individuellement, les différents VJ pouvaient programmer les réservoirs du club en plein air et en jouer de manière visuelle.

Dopo il successo di „Kubik" a Berlino i cubi illuminati hanno attratto allo stesso tempo un grande pubblico anche a Barcellona e Lisbona. 270 serbatoi d'acqua tradizionali da 1000 litri sono stati attrezzati per l'occasione con dispositivi di illuminazione ed erano così riconoscibili già da lontano. Tramite lampade pilotabili singolarmente diversi VJ hanno potuto „programmare" i serbatoi d'acqua dell'Open-Air-Club e così proiettarli visivamente.

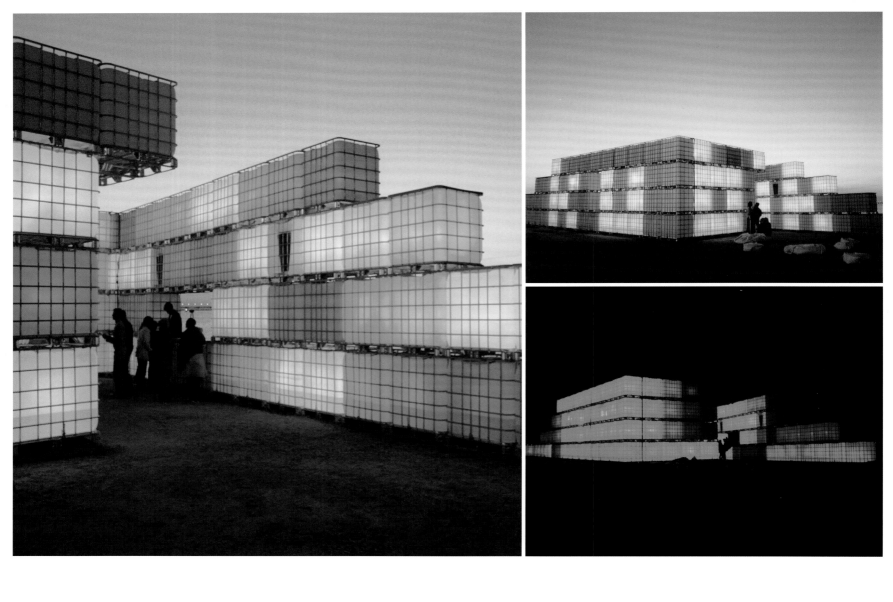

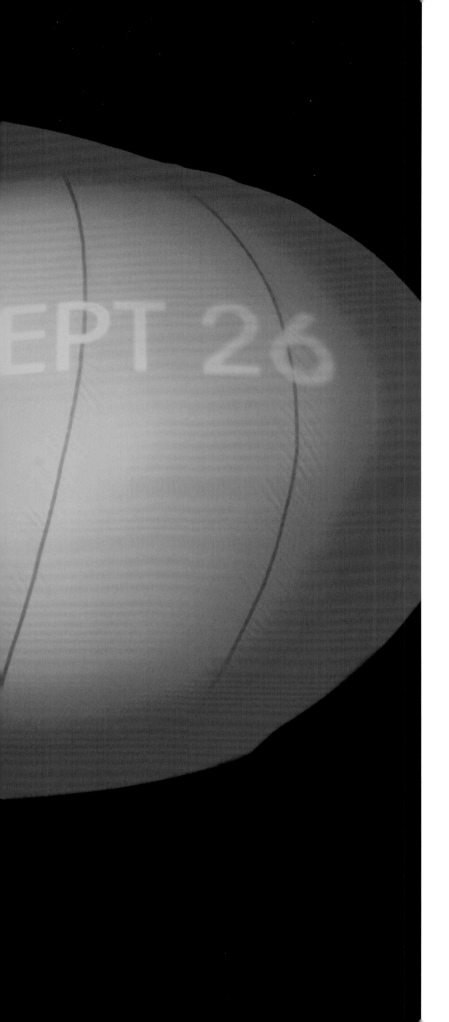

PHOCUS BRAND CONTACT | NUREMBERG
MICE Concept 26, Crossing the line.
Nuremberg, Germany | 27 April 2005
Photos: Johannes Paffrath

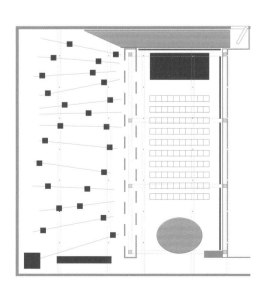

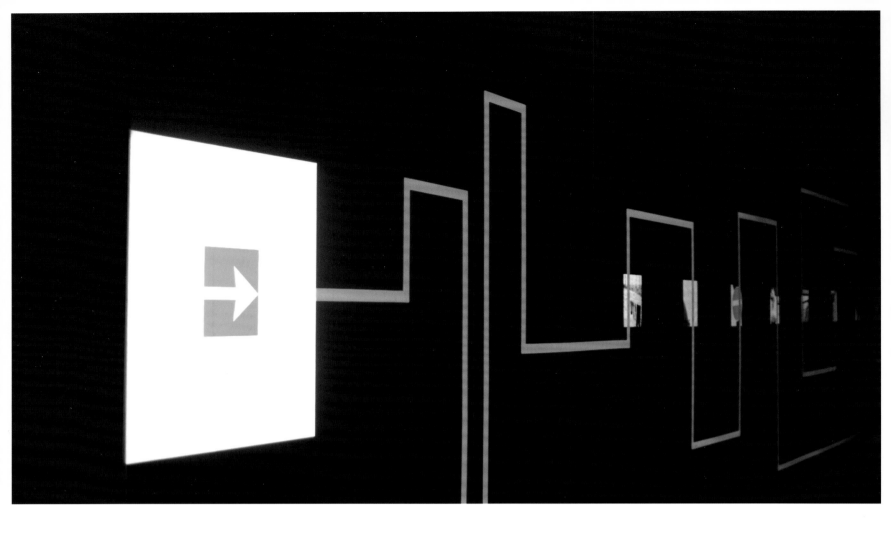

At **MICE agency's corporate event**, the guest-reception area and the bar had a black interior. In a consciously selected contrast to this, the infotainment area was presented behind white air-cushion curtains completely in white. Screens with media productions introduced the members of the agency; the "cloud" symbolized the world of ideas and the necessary freedom for creativity.

Beim Corporate Event der Agentur MICE waren Gästeempfang und Bar in schwarzem Interieur gehalten. In bewusst gewähltem Kontrast dazu präsentierte sich der Infotainmentbereich hinter weißen Luftpolstervorhängen ganz in Weiß. Bildschirme mit medialen Inszenierungen stellten die Mitarbeiter der Agentur dar; die „Wolke" symbolisierte die Gedankenwelt und den nötigen Freiraum für Kreativität.

En el evento corporativo de la agencia MICE, el interior de la zona de recepción de invitados y del bar era negro. En un contraste totalmente voluntario, el área de "infoentretenimiento" aparecía en blanco tras unas cortinas hinchables también blancas. Por medio de videocreaciones, unas pantallas mostraban a los miembros de la agencia. La nube simbolizaba el mundo de las ideas y el necesario espacio para la creatividad.

Lors de la soirée d'entreprise de l'agence MICE, la zone de réception des invités et le bar étaient habillés de noir. Avec un contraste consciemment choisi, la zone infotainment était présentée derrière des rideaux blancs à coussins d'air, totalement en blanc. Des écrans diffusant des réalisations médias présentaient les membres de l'agence : le « nuage » symbolisait le monde des idées et la liberté nécessaire à la créativité.

In occasione del Corporate Event dell'agenzia MICE il ricevimento degli ospiti e il bar sono stati tenuti in un interno nero. In un contrasto con questo ambiente scelto intenzionalmente il settore di informazione e intrattenimento si è presentato tutto in bianco dietro a un sipario fatto di cuscini d'aria bianchi. Gli schermi con rappresentazioni mediatiche hanno rappresentato i collaboratori dell'agenzia; la „nuvola" ha simboleggiato il mondo dei pensieri e lo spazio necessario alla creatività.

PHOCUS BRAND CONTACT | NUREMBERG
Pleasure.Passion.Paint – Big Up Your Life.
Nuremberg, Germany | 8 May 2007
Photos: Steffen Wirtgen

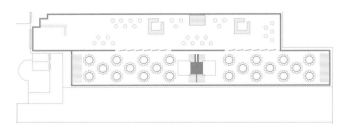

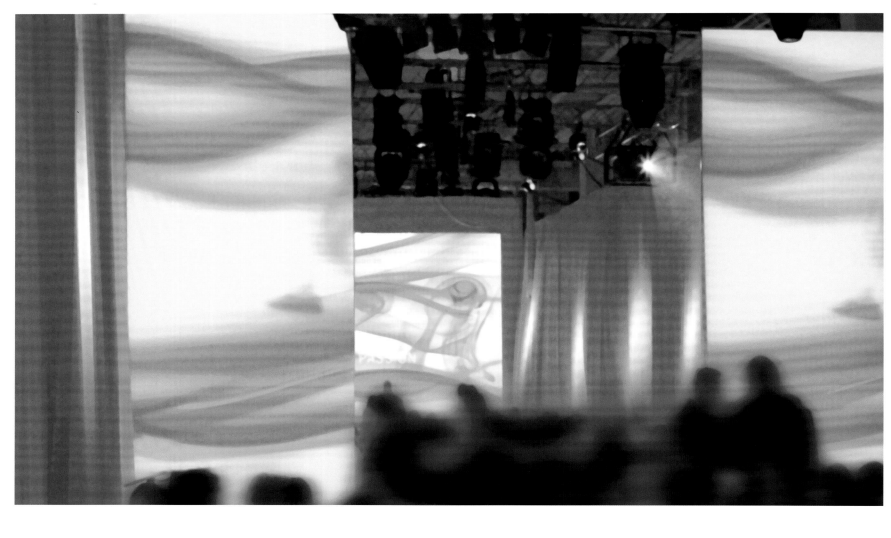

Parallel to the 2007 European Coatings Show (ECS), the mission was to document a media and artistic staging to support the positive perception of a chemical company's innovative power. Three show acts represented the motifs of product, application, and human being, bringing them together as the symbol of the event motto BIG UP YOUR LIFE in an impressive finale.

Während der Messe der Lack- und Farbenindustrie sollte durch eine mediale und künstlerische Inszenierung die positive Wahrnehmung einer Chemiefirma bezüglich ihrer Innovationskraft dokumentiert werden. Drei Showacts symbolisierten die Motive Produkt, Anwendung und Mensch und führten diese als Sinnbild des Veranstaltungsmottos BIG UP YOUR LIFE in einem beeindruckenden Finale zusammen.

Paralela a la edición de 2007 de la Feria Europea de la Pintura, el objetivo era crear un escenario mediático y artístico que avalara la percepción positiva de la capacidad de innovación de una firma química. Los actos se centraron en el producto, su aplicación y el ser humano, haciéndolos converger en un colofón impresionante con el lema del evento: BIG UP YOUR LIFE.

Parallèlement à l'édition 2007 de l'European Coatings Show (ECS), la mission était de mettre en place un support média et artistique pour soutenir la perception positive du pouvoir innovateur d'une entreprise chimique. Trois actes d'un spectacle représentaient le produit, les applications et l'être humain, les réunissant comme le symbole du leitmotiv de l'événement BIG UP YOUR LIFE dans un final impressionnant.

Parallelamente alla European Coatings Show (ECS) 2007 doveva venir documentata la percezione positiva di una ditta chimica in riferimento alla sua forza innovativa tramite una rappresentazione mediatica e artistica. I tre atti dello spettacolo hanno simboleggiato i motivi prodotto, utilizzo e uomo e li hanno riuniti in forma di simbolo del motto della manifestazione BIG UP YOUR LIFE in un finale sorprendente.

PLEASURE.PASSION.PAINT
BIG UP YOUR LIFE

PHOCUS BRAND CONTACT | NUREMBERG
Siemens Medical Solutions, Are you ready for Tim?
Nuremberg, Germany | 10 October 2005
Photos: Johannes Paffrath

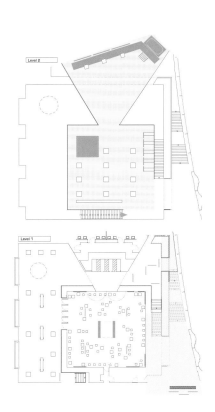

Get ready for a revolution

Siemens Medical Solutions extended an invitation to an exclusive evening event at the New Museum of Nuremberg for the worldwide product launch of the magnet-resonance technology Tim, which makes it possible to image the entire body at one time in a single examination. Up until the revelation of what "Tim" is, the PR department abstained from any type of concrete information—and the effect on the market was even greater as a result.

Zur weltweiten Produkteinführung der Magnetresonanztechnologie Tim, die erstmals Ganzkörperaufnahmen in einer einzigen Untersuchung ermöglicht, lud Siemens Medical Solutions zu einer exklusiven Abendveranstaltung ins Neue Museum Nürnberg. Bis zur Enthüllung, was „Tim" ist, verzichtete die PR-Abteilung auf jede Art von konkreter Information – umso größer war die Wirkung der Markteinführung.

Para la presentación mundial de la tecnología de resonancia magnética Tim, que permite por vez primera tomar imágenes de cuerpo entero en una sola exploración, Siemens Medical Solutions preparó una exclusiva velada en el Nuevo Museo de Núremberg. Hasta desvelar lo que era "Tim", el departamento de relaciones públicas se abstuvo de dar cualquier tipo de información para que la repercusión en el mercado aún fuera mayor.

Siemens Medical Solutions a prolongé une invitation à une soirée exclusive au Nouveau Musée de Nuremberg pour le lancement mondial de la technologie à résonnance magnétique Tim, qui permet de créer une image du corps entier en une fois lors d'un seul examen. Jusqu'à la révélation de ce qu'était « Tim », le département RP n'a fourni aucune information concrète, avec pour résultat un effet encore plus important sur le marché.

Per l'introduzione a livello mondiale del prodotto di tecnologia della risonanza magnetica Tim, che consente per la prima volta la ripresa dell'intero corpo in una singola visita, la Siemens Medical Solutions ha invitato i suoi ospiti a una rappresentazione serale al Museo Nuovo di Norimberga. Fino alla rivelazione cosa fosse la „Tim" il reparto PR ha rinunciato a qualsiasi tipo di informazione concreta - questo ha aumentato tanto più l'effetto dell'introduzione sul mercato.

EMSP GMBH/BRUCE B. GMBH | STUTTGART
SCHOKOLADE FILMPRODUKTION GMBH | STUTTGART
RECARO GmbH & Co. KG
100th year birthday celebration, Getting Closer
Stuttgart, Germany | 29 April 2006
Photos: Zooey Braun (p 204, 207 top, 208 left), Volker Dreixler

For its 100-year anniversary, the RECARO GmbH & Co. KG presented itself to its international guests using various theme rooms. In the banquet hall itself, six screens served as a multimedia stage setting that showed the event logo, the opening trailer, the speaker trailer, and the main film—Getting Closer. The film had a three-dimensional effect and integrated the event location into the production.

Zu ihrem 100jährigen Jubiläum präsentierte sich die RECARO GmbH & Co. KG ihren internationalen Gästen anhand diverser Themenräume. Im Festsaal selbst dienten sechs Leinwände als multimediales Bühnenbild. Es zeigte das Veranstaltungslogo, den Eröffnungstrailer, Rednertrailer und den Hauptfilm „Getting Closer". Der Film arbeitete dreidimensional und bezog den Veranstaltungsort in die Inszenierung mit ein.

Con motivo de su centenario, RECARO GmbH & Co. KG se presentó ante sus invitados de todo el mundo en diferentes espacios temáticos. En el mismo salón, seis pantallas hicieron las veces de escenario multimedia. En ellas se mostraron el logotipo del acto, el vídeo de inauguración, otros con varios oradores y el corto principal, "Getting Closer", un vídeo tridimensional en el que el propio recinto tomó parte en la puesta en escena.

Pour son 100ème anniversaire, RECARO Gmbh & Co.KG s'est présenté à ses invités venus du monde entier à travers diverses pièces à thèmes. Dans la salle de banquet, six écrans servaient de scène multimédia affichant le logo de la soirée, la bande-annonce d'ouverture, la bande-annonce audio, et le film principal – Getting Closer. Le film disposait d'effets 3D, et intégrait le lieu de la soirée dans la projection.

In occasione del suo giubileo dei 100 anni la RECARO GmbH & Co. KG si è presentata ai suoi ospiti internazionali attraverso diverse sale a tema. Nel salone delle feste stesso c'erano sei tele che servivano da scenografia multimediale. Si è mostrato il logo della manifestazione, il trailer di apertura, il trailer del relatore e il film principale „Getting Closer". Il film era rappresentato tridimensionalmente e ha inglobato nella messa in scena il luogo della manifestazione.

SPY | ISTANBUL
Bridgestone Sabanci Lastik San. ve Tic. A.S.
Lassa SNOWAYS Event
Various locations in Sweden, mainly Jukkäsjarvi | 2007
Photos: Mufit Cirpanli

The Turkish tire manufacturer Lassa – which belongs to the Bridgestone Concern – invited adventurous winners on a three-day event in the high north at the conclusion of a lottery promotion. The program included a ride on a dogsled from the airport to camp, a test drive with the new Snoways 2 Plus tires at minus 31 degrees F, and accommodations at a specially designed ice hotel.

Nach einer Lotto-Aktion hat der zum Bridgestone-Konzern gehörende türkische Reifenhersteller Lassa die abenteuerlustigen Gewinner zu einem dreitägigen Event im hohen Norden eingeladen. Auf dem Programm standen eine Fahrt im Hundeschlitten vom Flughafen zum Camp, eine Testfahrt mit den neuen Snoways 2 Plus-Reifen bei Minus 35 Grad und die Unterbringung im eigens entworfenen Eishotel.

Lassa, fabricante turco de neumáticos perteneciente a la multinacional Bridgestone, invitó a los aguerridos ganadores de un sorteo a un evento de tres días en zonas árticas. El programa incluyó viajar en trineos tirados por perros desde el aeropuerto al punto de destino, probar los nuevos neumáticos Snoways-2-Plus a 35 bajo cero y pernoctar en el hotel de hielo que ellos mismos habían diseñado.

Le fabricant de pneus turc Lassa – qui appartient au Consortium Bridgestone – a invité les audacieux gagnants de sa loterie à un voyage de trois jours dans le grand nord. Le programme incluait une virée sur un traîneau à chiens de l'aéroport au camp, un tour d'essai avec les nouveaux pneus Snoways 2 Plus à - 35 degrés, et un hébergement dans un hôtel de glace spécialement conçu pour l'occasion.

Dopo una azione del lotto il produttore di pneumatici turco Lassa, facente parte del complesso della Bridgestone, ha invitato i vincitori avventurosi a un evento nel Nord della durata di tre giorni. Il programma prevedeva una gita con i cani da slitta dall'aeroporto al Camp, un giro di prova con i nuovi pneumatici Snoways 2 Plus a una temperatura di meno 35 gradi e la sistemazione in un albergo di ghiaccio progettato appositamente.

THE EVENT COMPANY | MUNICH

Europa-Fachpresse-Verlag
W&V Meetnight
Munich, Germany | 12 May 2005
Photos: Fabrice dall'Anese

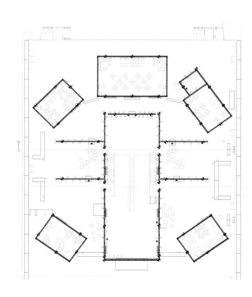

The annual networking event of the communications sector was held under the motto of "Trusting in Brands"—for ninety minutes, not one single logo or branding could be seen in the Munich event arena—not on the bars, bottles, or glasses, and not even on the personal objects belonging to the guests. The solution finally came through an audiovisual staging of the participating sponsors' brands.

Das jährliche Networking-Event der Kommunikationsbranche stand unter dem Motto „Vertrauen in Marken" – neunzig Minuten lang war in der Münchner Eventarena kein einziges Logo oder Branding zu sehen. Nicht auf Bars, Flaschen oder Gläsern, nicht einmal auf den persönlichen Gegenständen der Gäste. Über eine audiovisuelle Inszenierung der beteiligten Sponsoren-Marken erfolgte schließlich die Auflösung.

El "networking-event" anual del mundo de la comunicación tuvo lugar este año bajo el lema "confianza en las marcas": durante noventa minutos no se vio en el Eventarena de Múnich ni un solo logotipo o marca. Ni en bares, botellas ni vasos, ni siquiera en los objetos personales de los invitados. Un espectáculo audiovisual por parte de las marcas patrocinadoras terminó desvelándolas.

Le Networking Event annuel de l'industrie de la communication a été organisé sous le slogan « Croire en les marques » - pendant quatre-vingt-dix minutes, on ne pouvait pas voir la moindre marque ou logo dans l'enceinte de l'événement à Munich – ni sur les bars, les bouteilles ou les verres, ni même sur les objets personnels des invités. La solution est finalement arrivée avec une mise en scène audiovisuelle des marques sponsors participantes.

L'evento annuale sul Networking del settore della comunicazione è stata posto sotto il motto „Fiducia nelle marche" – per novanta minuti nella Eventarena di Monaco non si è visto né un logo né un marchio. Non c'erano sui bar, sulle bottiglie o sui bicchieri, e neanche sugli oggetti personali degli ospiti. Attraverso una messa in scena visuale delle marche sponsor è stato infine rivelata la soluzione.

THE EVENT COMPANY | MUNICH
Pioneer Investments
Faces of a new company
Munich, Germany | 16 November 2006
Photos: Michael Namberger, Christine Schaum

The employee event was a milestone in the fusion of Pioneer Investments and Activest. Instead of big speeches, the event concept relied on symbolic gestures to create a "we feeling." An outsized Pioneer logo was created from the 350 employee pictures. The size and the values of the company were communicated during dinner on 12 large projections.

Ein Meilenstein bei der Fusion von Pioneer Investments und Activest war der Mitarbeiterevent. Statt auf große Reden setzte das Eventkonzept auf symbolische Gesten, um ein Wir-Gefühl zu schaffen. Aus 350 Mitarbeiterbildern entstand ein überdimensionaler Pioneer-Schriftzug. Beim Abendessen wurden auf 12 großen Projektionen die Größe und die Werte des Unternehmens kommuniziert.

El acto para los empleados celebrado tras la fusión de Pioneer Invest-ments y Activest marcó todo un hito. En lugar de darle protagonismo a los discursos, se le dio a los gestos simbólicos para crear un sentimiento de unidad. 350 fotos de empleados conformaron un gigantesco letrero con las letras de Pioneer. Durante la cena, la dimensión y los valores de la empresa se transmitieron por medio de 12 inmensas proyecciones.

La soirée des employés était l'événement clé de la fusion de Pioneer Investments et d'Activest. Plutôt que sur des grands discours, le concept de la soirée était basé sur des gestes symboliques pour créer un « senti-ment d'appartenance ». Un logo Pioneer démesuré a été créé à partir des photos de 350 employés. La dimension et les valeurs de la compagnie ont été communiquées pendant le dîner sur 12 vastes projections.

L'evento dei collaboratori è stato una pietra miliare della fusione di Pioneer Investments con Activest. Invece di presentarsi con grandi parole il concetto dell'evento ha puntato su gesti simbolici per creare la sensa-zione del Noi. Da 350 foto di collaboratori è scaturito un tratto di scrittura surdimensionale della Pioneer. Durante la cena sono stati comunicati la grandezza e i valori dell'azienda su 12 grandi proiezioni.

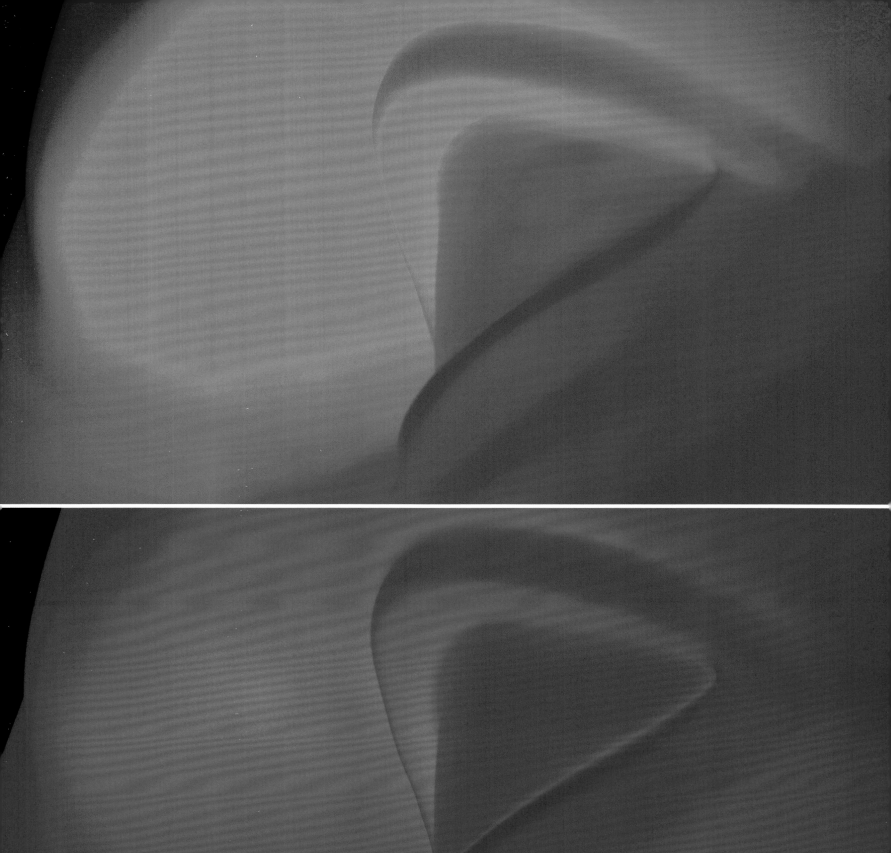

TOTEMS | COMMUNICATION & ARCHITECTURE | STUTTGART
LGT Group, Brand Dinner
Vaduz, Lichtenstein | 18 January 2005
Photos: Ilja Knezovic, visuarte

"Uniqueness" was the expectation of the LGT Bank for its new corporate design. As a result, the Totems agency staged a metamorphosis during a dinner for 80 top managers. Beginning with the interchangeability of the competition, the new clear design of the LGT Bank emerged at the end of the transformation. The walls of the room became artistic communication surfaces via projections.

„Einzigartigkeit" war der Anspruch der LGT Bank an ihr neues Corporate Design. Dafür inszenierte die Agentur Totems während eines Abendessens für 80 Top-Manager eine Metamorphose. Angefangen bei der Austauschbarkeit der Konkurrenz stand am Ende der Verwandlung das neue klare Design der LGT Bank. Die Wände des Raums wurden dabei via Projektionen zur künstlerischen Kommunikationsfläche.

"Único" fue el lema del nuevo diseño corporativo del LGT Bank. La agencia Totems preparó para este fin una metamorfosis durante la cena que ofreció a 80 cuadros directivos. Mientras que la competencia apenas se diferencia, al final de esta transformación se divisaba el nuevo e inconfundible diseño del LGT Bank. Valiéndose de unas artísticas proyecciones, las paredes del recinto se convirtieron en áreas comunicativas.

« Unique », c'était ce qu'attendait la Banque LGT de son nouveau design d'entreprise. L'agence Totems a donc mis en scène une métamorphose pendant un dîner pour ses 80 plus grands managers. Après un début montrant le caractère interchangeable de la compétition, le nouveau design clair de la Banque LGT a émergé à la fin de la transformation. Via des projections, les murs de la pièce sont devenus des surfaces de communication artistique.

„Unicità" è stata la pretesa della banca LGT rivolta al nuovo Corporate Design. Per questo l'agenzia Totems ha inscenato durante la cena una metamorfosi per 80 Top-Manager. A iniziare dall' intercambiabilità della concorrenza alla fine della metamorfosi si è presentato il nuovo chiaro design della banca LGT. In tale occasione le pareti della sala si sono trasformate tramite proiezioni in una superficie di comunicazione artistica.

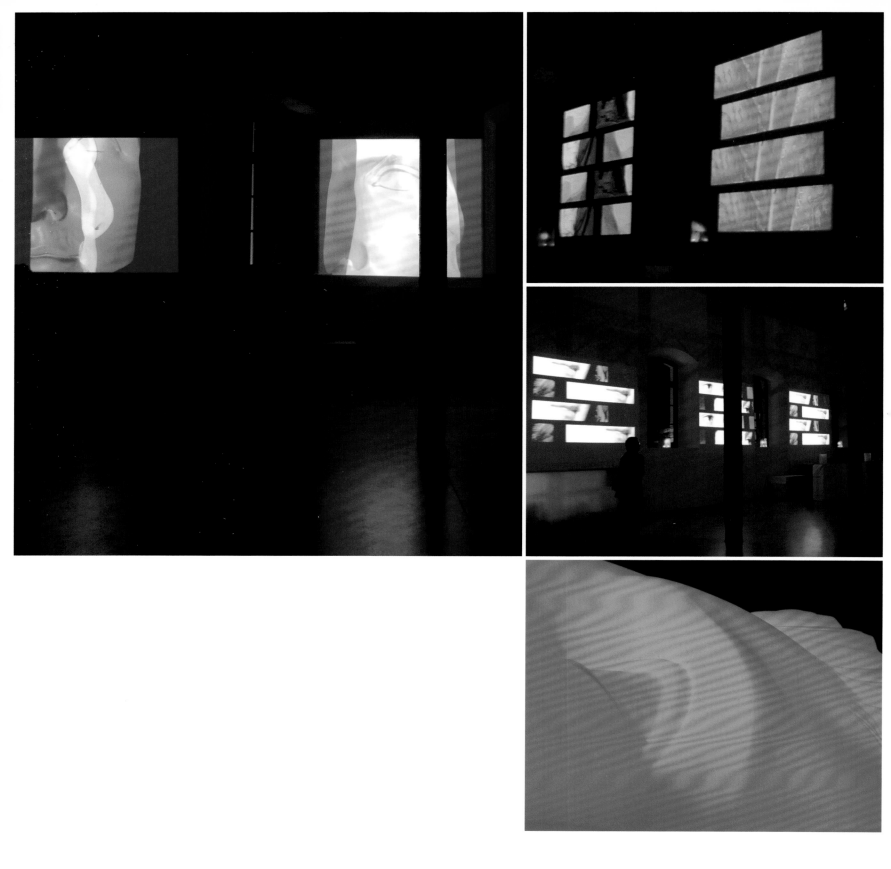

TRIAD | BERLIN
KarstadtQuelle AG
Jubilee night „Neue Wege gehen"
Berlin, Germany | 20 May 2006
Photos: Bernd Brundert, © Triad Berlin

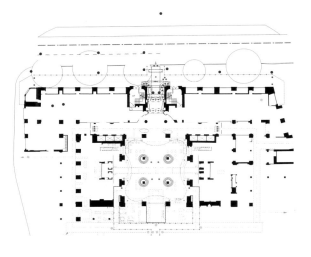

For the 125th anniversary of Karstadt, Triad Berlin turned the atrium of the KaDeWe into a large show stage. A living doll above the entrance welcomed the arriving guests. The highlight was a choreographed fashion show with dancers of the Berlin State Ballet: Four upcoming new designers presented their collections on two illluminated catwalks that were lowered.

Für das 125-jährige Jubiläum von Karstadt verwandelte Triad Berlin das Atrium des KaDeWe in eine große Showbühne. Eine Living Doll über dem Eingang begrüßte die ankommenden Gäste. Höhepunkt war eine choreographierte Modenschau mit Tänzern des Berliner Staatsballetts: Auf zwei Illuminierten Laufstegen, die herabgesenkt wurden, präsentierten vier Nachwuchs-Designer ihre Kollektionen.

Por el 125 aniversario de Karstadt Triad Berlin convirtió el atrio de los grandes almacenes KaDeWe en un gigantesco escenario. Una muñeca viviente le daba la bienvenida a los invitados. El momento culminante vino con el desfile de modelos por parte de los bailarines del Ballet de Berlín que se desarrolló sobre dos pasarelas móviles que bajaron hasta el suelo. En ellas presentaron sus colecciones cuatro nuevos diseñadores.

Pour le 125ème anniversaire de Karstadt, Triad Berlin a transformé l'atrium du KaDeWe en une vaste scène. Au dessus de l'entrée, une poupée vivante accueillait les visiteurs. Le temps fort de la manifestation était un défilé de mode chorégraphié avec les danseurs du Ballet National de Berlin. Quatre jeunes designers ont présenté leurs collections sur deux passerelles illuminées et surbaissées.

In occasione del giubileo dei 125 anni della Karstadt la Triad Berlin ha trasformato l'atrio del KaDeWe in un grande palcoscenico. Una bambola vivente sopra l'ingresso ha salutato gli ospiti al loro arrivo. Il punto culminante è stata la sfilata coreografica con ballerini del corpo di ballo statale di Berlino: su due passerelle illuminate, che sono state abbassate, quattro giovani designer dell'ultima generazione hanno presentato le loro collezioni.

TRIAD | BERLIN
Alfred Herrhausen Gesellschaft
Urban Age Summit „Im Zeitalter der Städte"
Berlin, Germany | 10 November 2006
Photos: Bernd Brundert, © Triad Berlin

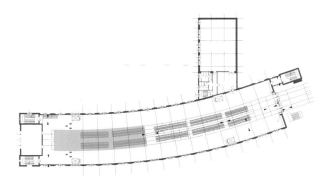

The Urban Age Summit in Berlin is the conclusion of an international conference series on the topic of the "Age of the City." At the evening event in the Postbahnhof, white models of the individual conference cities staged by light produced a thematic connection to the conference program. The successful interplay of architecture, exhibition objects, and light dramaturgy created a stylish atmosphere.

Der Urban Age Summit in Berlin bildete den Abschluss einer internationalen Konferenzreihe zum Thema „Zeitalter der Städte". Bei der Abendveranstaltung im Postbahnhof stellten lichtinszenierte Weißmodelle zu einzelnen Konferenz-Metropolen eine thematische Verbindung zum Tagungsprogramm her. Das gelungene Zusammenspiel von Architektur, Ausstellungsobjekten und Lichtdramaturgie schuf eine stilvolle Atmosphäre.

Con la Urban Age Summit se clausuraron en Berlín unas jornadas sobre la "Era de las ciudades". En la velada celebrada en la estación de Postbahnhof, unas maquetas blancas dotadas de iluminación de las urbes protagonistas de la conferencia sirvieron de hilo conductor. Una combinación muy lograda de arquitectura, piezas de exposición y dramaturgia luminosa dio lugar a una atmósfera muy elegante.

Le Sommet Urban Age de Berlin est la conclusion d'une série de conférences internationales sur le thème « L'Age de la Ville ». Lors de la soirée au Postbahnhof, des maquettes blanches des différentes villes évoquées ont été illuminées dans une mise en scène établissant une connexion avec le programme de conférences. L'interaction réussie entre l'architecture, les objets exposés et la dramaturgie lumineuse a permis de créer une atmosphère élégante.

L'Urban Age Summit a Berlin ha costituito la conclusione di una sequenza di conferenze sul tema „L'età delle città". Durante la manifestazione serale presso la stazione postale alcuni modelli in bianco messi in scena con effetti luminosi in relazione a singole metropoli delle conferenze hanno rappresentato un collegamento tematico con il programma del convegno. L'interazione riuscita tra architettura, oggetti esposti e drammaturgia luminosa ha creato un'atmosfera di stile.

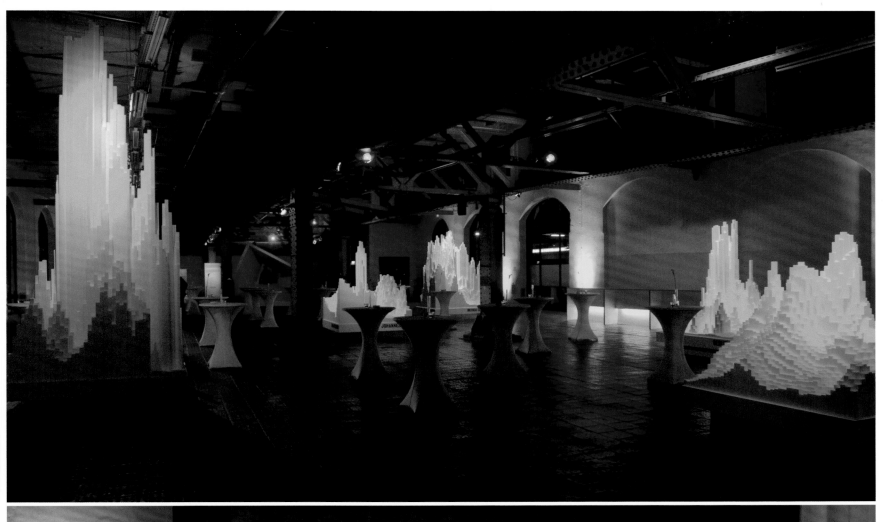
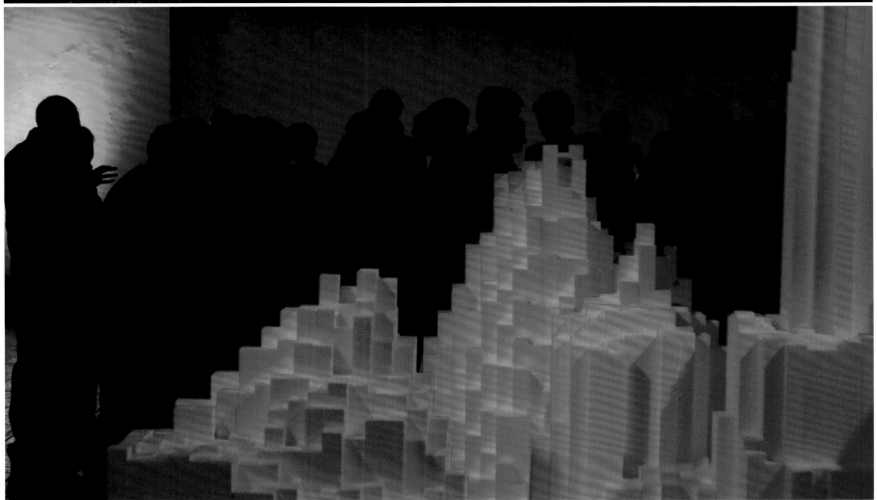

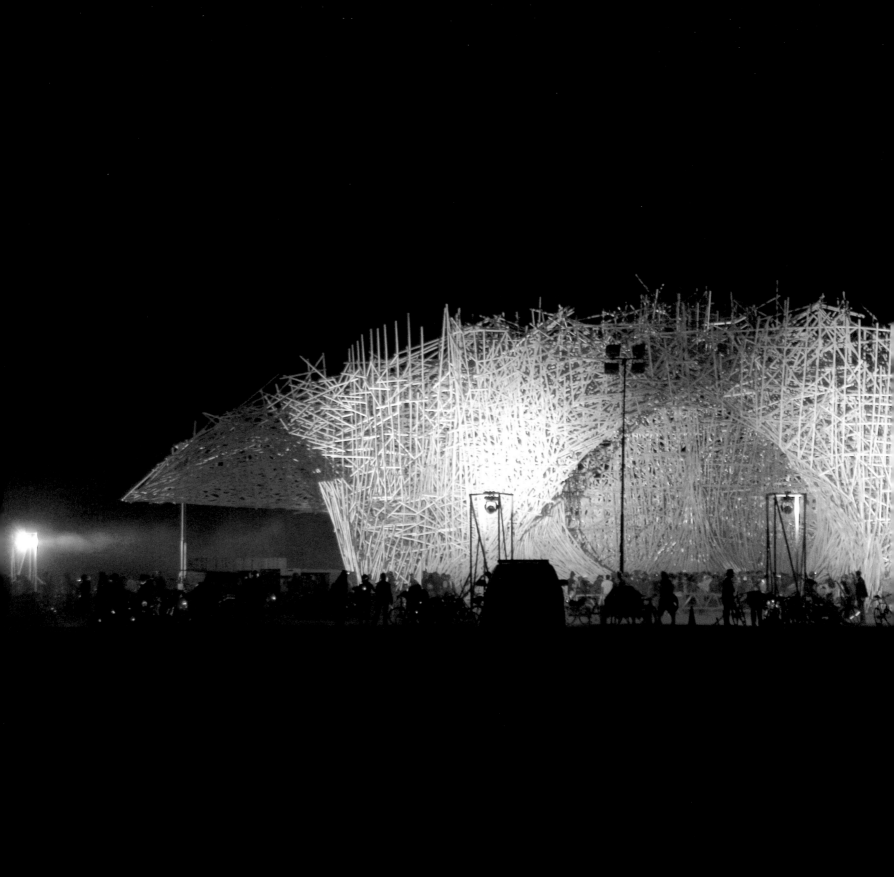

THE UCHRONIANS | DIVERSE
WITH JAN KRIEKELS AND ARNE QUINZE
Installation at the burning man festival
Black Rock City, USA | Summer 2006
Photos: Marc Vonstein, Thierry van Dort,
Uchronians, www.uchronians.org

253

For the Burning Man Festival in Black Rock City/Nevada, 43 people worked for 13 days to build Uchronia. The result was a construction of scrap wood that was spectacularly illuminated at times and covered an area of 197 × 99 feet. Its construction and later burning was intended to symbolize the beginning of a creative, new type of approach to business that also takes nature into consideration.

Für das Burning Man Festival in Black Rock City in Nevada bauten 43 Personen 13 Tage lang „Uchronia". Das Ergebnis war eine zeitweise spektakulär beleuchtete Konstruktion aus Abfallholz, die eine Fläche von 60 × 30 Metern bedeckte. Der Bau und seine spätere Verbrennung sollten den Beginn eines kreativen und neuartigen Wirtschaftens symbolisieren, das auch die Natur berücksichtigt.

Durante el Festival Burning Man de Black Rock City, en Nevada (EE. UU.), 43 personas invirtieron 13 días en construir "Uchronia". El resultado fue una espectacular obra de madera dotada de iluminación y que cubría una superficie de 60 x 30 metros. Su construcción y su posterior quema simbolizaron el inicio de una forma de negocio creativa y novedosa, al tiempo que respetuosa con la naturaleza.

Pour le Festival Burning Man de Black Rock dans le Nevada, 43 personnes ont travaillé pendant 13 jours pour bâtir « Uchronia ». Le résultat était une construction en retailles de bois, qui était illuminée ponctuellement de manière spectaculaire et couvrait une zone de 60 × 30 mètres. Sa construction puis sa crémation se voulaient le symbole du commencement d'une nouvelle approche créative des affaires qui prendrait la nature en considération.

In occasione del Burning Man Festival a Black Rock City in Nevada 43 persone hanno costruito per 13 giorni il „Uchronia". Il risultato è stata una costruzione di tanto in tanto illuminata in modo spettacolare e costituita da legno di scarto, per una superficie di 60 × 30 metri. La costruzione e la sua successiva messa al rogo dovevano simboleggiare l'inizio di un'amministrazione creativa e nuova che rispetti anche la natura.

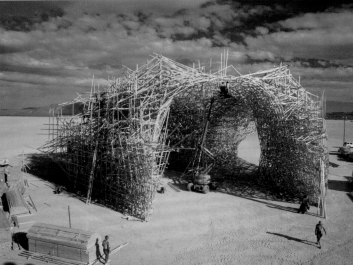

VELUM INTERMEDIA | STUTTGART
Honda Motor Europe, CR-V Press Test Drive
Barcelona, Spain | 2006
Photos: velum intermedia GmbH

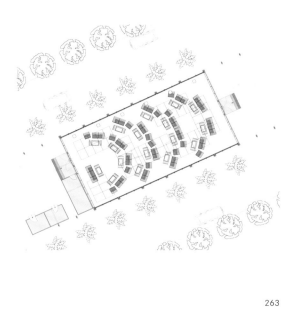

The new Honda CR-V was introduced to the international press in the direct vicinity of the Barcelona Airport in a transparent pavilion of wood and glass. A lounge for the technical presentation of the new vehicle was created on the inside of the building. All of the contents related to the car were presented to the journalists through flat monitors built into the couch tables.

In direkter Nähe zum Flughafen Barcelona stellte Honda den neuen CR-V in einem transparenten Pavillon aus Holz und Glas der internationalen Presse vor. Im Inneren diente eine ansprechende Lounge zur technischen Präsentation des neuen Autos. Die Inhalte rund um das Fahrzeug wurden den Journalisten durch in die Couchtische eingelassene Flachbildschirme vermittelt.

El nuevo Honda CR-V se presentó a la prensa internacional en un pabellón transparente de madera y cristal en las inmediaciones del aeropuerto de Barcelona. En su interior se acondicionó una sala para la presentación técnica del nuevo vehículo. Toda la información referente al mismo le fue transmitida a los periodistas a través de unas pantallas planas insertadas en las mesas.

La nouvelle Honda CR-V a été présentée à la presse internationale tout près de l'aéroport de Barcelone dans un pavillon transparent de bois et de verre. Un salon pour la présentation technique du nouveau véhicule a été créé à l'intérieur du bâtiment. Toutes les informations relatives à la voiture étaient présentées aux journalistes grâce à des moniteurs plats intégrés dans les tables basses.

La nuova Honda CR-V è stata presentata alla stampa internazionale in prossimità dell'aeroporto di Barcellona in un padiglione trasparente fatto di legno e vetro. All'interno è stata creata una lounge per la presentazione tecnica della nuova autovettura. Tramite degli schermi piatti incassati nei tavolini da salotto i giornalisti sono stati informati di tutti i contenuti riguardanti il veicolo.

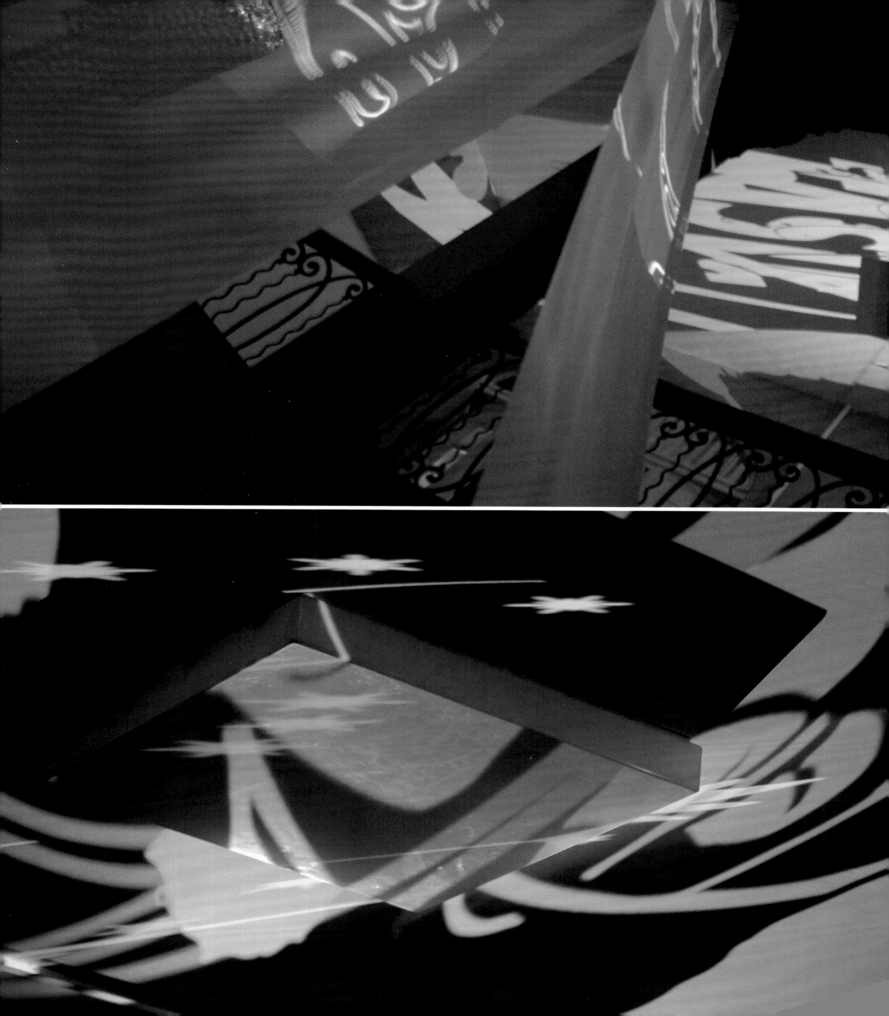

VISUARTE | STUTTGART
Lucky Strike, Discover taste 2006
Stuttgart, Germany | 2006
Photos: Ilja Knezovic, visuarte

The agency visuarte staged an event for the introduction of two new Lucky Strike tastes. The graphic style elements of the products served as the model for the media playing on the architecture. This was implemented with the help of video and slide projectors.

Die Agentur visuarte inszenierte das Event zur Einführung zweier neuer Geschmacksrichtungen von Lucky Strike. Die graphischen Stilelemente der Produkte dienten als Vorlage für die mediale Bespielung der Architektur, welche mit Hilfe von Video- und Diaprojektoren umgesetzt wurde.

La agencia Visuarte organizó un acto para presentar dos nuevos sabores de Lucky Strike. Los elementos gráficos y estilísticos de los productos sirvieron de modelo para la interactuación de la arquitectura. Para ello se recurrió a la utilización de proyecciones de vídeo y diapositivas.

L'agence Visuarte a mis en scène un événement pour le lancement de deux nouveaux goûts de Lucky Strike. Les éléments graphiques des produits ont servi de modèle pour le jeu des médias sur l'architecture. La mise en scène s'est faite à l'aide de vidéos et de projecteurs coulissants.

L'agenzia Visuarte ha allestito l'evento per l'introduzione di due nuove tendenza del gusto della Lucky Strike. Gli elementi di stile grafici dei prodotti fungevano da presentazione della rappresentazione mediatica dell'architettura che è stata trasformata con l'aiuto di videoproiettori e di proiettori per diapositive.

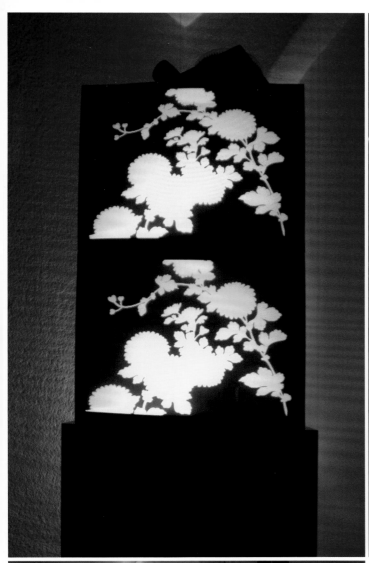

Willkommen in der Bilfinger Berger City
Welcome to Bilfinger Berger City

The Multi Service Group   BILFINGER BERGER

VOSS+FISCHER
MARKETING EVENT AGENTUR GMBH | FRANKFURT
Bilfinger Berger AG, 125 jubilee celebration
Mannheim, Germany | 24 – 26 June 2005
Photos: VOSS+FISCHER

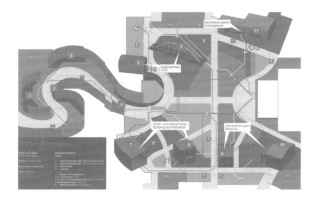

Die Harmonie perfekter Dienstleistung The...

Alte Oper in Frankfurt –
Bühne für hochkarätige Events
Alte Oper in Frankfurt –
Setting the stage for top-flight events

For its 125th company anniversary, the construction company Bilfinger Berger AG invited about 3,000 guests over three days to a building that was exclusively set up temporarily for this occasion on Maimarkt (May Market) site in Mannheim. In the Bilfinger Berger City, architectural highlights from the past illustrated the long path to success and current structures demonstrated the present spectrum of achievements by the Bilfinger Berger company.

Zum 125jährigen Firmenjubiläum lud das Bauunternehmen Bilfinger Berger AG an drei Tagen rund 3000 Gäste in einen temporären, zu diesem Anlass exklusiv errichteten Bau auf dem Maimarktgelände in Mannheim. In der „Bilfinger Berger City" verdeutlichten bauliche Highlights aus der Vergangenheit den langen Erfolgsweg, aktuelle Bauten demonstrierten das Leistungsspektrum des Unternehmens Bilfinger Berger von heute.

En el 125 aniversario de la empresa, la constructora Bilfinger Berger AG invitó a unas 3.000 personas a pasar tres días en una edificación en el Maimarkt (el mercado de mayo) de Mannheim, levantada ex profeso para esta celebración. En la "Ciudad Bilfinger Berger", los hitos arquitectónicos pasados ilustraron el largo camino hacia el éxito, mientras que las construcciones actuales mostraban el espectro actual de sus logros.

Pour son 125ème anniversaire, l'entreprise de construction Bilfinger Berger AG a invité environ 3000 personnes pendant trois jours dans un bâtiment construit exclusivement et temporairement pour cette occasion sur le site de Maimarkt (Marché de Mai) à Mannheim. Dans la ville de Bilfinger Berger, des attractions architecturales du passé illustraient le long chemin vers le succès et les structures actuelles déployaient l'éventail des réussites actuelles de la société Bilfinger Berger.

In occasione del giubileo dei 125 anni della ditta l'impresa di costruzioni Bilfinger Berger AG ha invitato nell'arco di tre giorni circa 3000 ospiti in una costruzione temporanea, costruita appositamente per questa occasione nell'area del Maimarkt (mercato di maggio) a Mannheim. Nella „Bilfinger Berger City" gli apogei costruttivi del passato hanno esposto la lunga via verso il successo, mentre delle costruzioni d'attualità hanno testimoniato lo spettro delle prestazioni di oggi dell'impresa Bilfinger Berger.

Britische Botschaft Berlin

Betreiberprojekte
Concessions

Im Rahmen von Betreibermodellen übernehmen private Unternehmen die Verantwortung für Planung, Finanzierung, Erstellung und langjährigen Betrieb von öffentlicher Infrastruktur. Bilfinger Berger konzentriert sich auf Verkehrsprojekte und den öffentlichen Hochbau. Die wichtigsten Märkte sind Australien und Großbritannien. Mit seinem umfassenden Know-how ist der Konzern auch auf dem sich entwickelnden deutschen Markt hervorragend positioniert.

Within the context of concession projects, private businesses take on the responsibility for the design, funding and the long-term operation of public infrastructure facilities. Bilfinger Berger focuses on transportation infrastructure projects and public buildings. Australia and Great Britain are among the company's main markets, and Bilfinger Berger is also ideally positioned as the growing German market starts to be competitive in nature.

1919

1939

1950

Alles unter Kontrolle
Everything under control

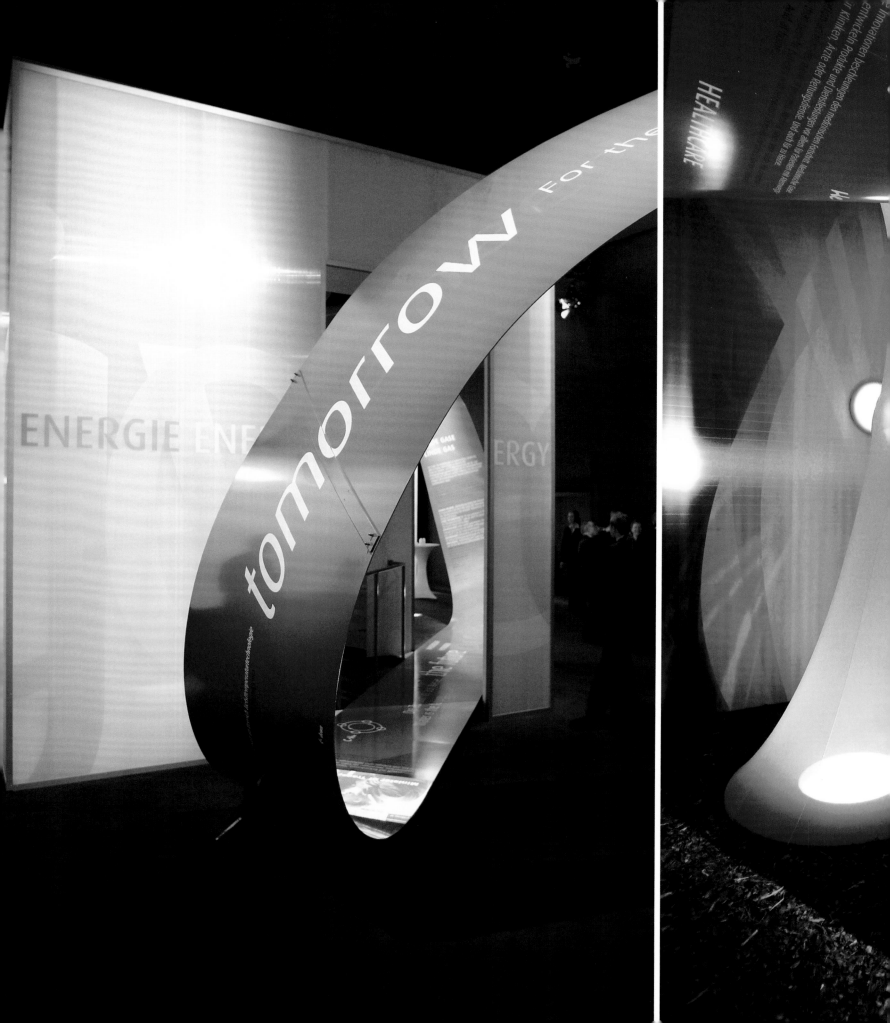

VOSS+FISCHER
MARKETING EVENT AGENTUR GMBH | FRANKFURT
Linde AG, 125 jubilee celebration
Hoellriegelskreuth/Munich, Germany | 24 June 2004
Photos: VOSS+FISCHER

For its 125th company anniversary, the Linde AG had a temporary building constructed on the employee parking lot in Höllriegelskreuth for about 1,000 invited guests. In the interior, 590 feet of steel curved through the space in company colors and told its history. In between, the blue boxes succinctly presented the company's competencies and prompted activities and questions as an adventure zone.

Zum 125jährigen Firmenjubiläum ließ die Linde AG auf dem Mitarbeiterparkplatz in Höllriegelskreuth einen temporären Bau für rund 1000 geladene Gäste errichten. Im Inneren wanden sich 180 m gebogener Stahl in der Farbe des Hauses und erzählten dessen Geschichte. Dazwischen brachten die Blue Boxes die Unternehmenskompetenzen auf den Punkt und regten als Erlebniszone zu Beschäftigung und Fragen an.

Con motivo de su 125 aniversario, la compañía Linde AG erigió en Höllriegelskreuth (Alemania) una edificación efímera para los cerca de 1.000 invitados. En su interior, una cinta de 180 metros de acero se extendía por la instalación en los colores de la empresa relatando su historia. La cruzaban grandes cajones azules que presentaban las áreas de la firma y que animaban a la actividad y a querer saber más.

Pour son 125ème anniversaire, Linde AG a fait construire un bâtiment temporaire sur le parking des employés à Höllriegelskreuth pour recevoir environ 1000 invités. A l'intérieur, 180 mètres d'acier aux couleurs de l'entreprise, serpentant à travers l'espace, racontaient son histoire. Les boîtes bleues présentaient succinctement les compétences de l'entreprise et suscitaient les activités et les questions, formant une zone d'aventure.

In occasione del giubileo dei 125 anni della ditta la Linde AG ha fatto erigere sul parcheggio dei dipendenti a Höllriegelskreuth una costruzione temporanea per circa 1000 invitati. All'interno si snodavano 180 m di acciaio curvato in tinta con la casa che ne hanno raccontato la storia. In mezzo c'erano le Blue Boxes che sottolineavano le competenze dell'azienda e stimolavano ad attività e domande in quanto zona di sperimentazione.

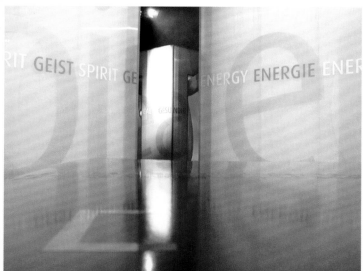

ZANDER & PARTNER EVENT MARKETING GMBH | BERLIN
City Stiftung Berlin, Festival of Lights
Berlin, Germany | 2006
Photos: Festival of Lights,
Panirama (Illumination p 286), Andreas Boehlke (Illumination
p 288-295), Theater des Westens (Illumination p 296)

During the last two weeks of October, many landmarks, buildings, streets, and squares of Berlin have been staged with light, events, projections, and fireworks during the Festival of Lights. Since 2005, this has transformed the capital city into a glittering metropolis. Spectacular examples of this are the Berlin Dom, the Brandenburger Tor, the Siegessäule, the Oberbaumbrücke bridge, and the Alte Museum.

Beim Festival of Lights werden seit 2005 immer in den letzten beiden Oktoberwochen viele Wahrzeichen, Gebäude, Straßen und Plätze Berlins mit Licht, Events, Projektionen und Feuerwerk in Szene gesetzt und die Hauptstadt so in eine Glitzermetropole verwandelt. Spektakuläre Beispiele dafür sind der Berliner Dom, das Brandenburger Tor, die Siegessäule, die Oberbaumbrücke und das Alte Museum.

Desde el año 2005, durante el Festival de las Luces de Berlín, que se celebra las dos últimas semanas de octubre, muchos símbolos, edificios, calles y plazas de esta ciudad se iluminan con luces, proyecciones o fuegos artificiales, transformando la ciudad en una deslumbrante metrópolis. Valgan como ejemplos espectaculares la Catedral de Berlín, la Puerta de Brandeburgo, la Torre de la Victoria, el Puente Oberbaum y el Altes Museum.

Pendant les deux dernières semaines d'Octobre, de nombreux sites, bâtiments, rues et parcs de Berlin ont été mis en valeur avec des illuminations, des manifestations, des projections et des feux d'artifice dans le cadre de la Fête des Lumières. Depuis 2005, elle a transformé la capitale en une métropole scintillante. Des exemples spectaculaires : le Berlin Dom, la Porte de Brandebourg, le Siegessäule, le Pont Oberbaumbrücke et l'Alte Museum.

In occasione del Festival of Lights dal 2005, sempre nelle ultime due settimane di ottobre, vengono rappresentati molti emblemi, edifici, strade e piazze di Berlino con luci, eventi, proiezioni e fuochi d'artificio e la capitale si trasforma così in una metropoli scintillante. Degli esempi spettacolari per questo sono il duomo di Berlino, la porta di Brandenburgo, la colonna della vittoria, il ponte Oberbaum e il Vecchio Museo.

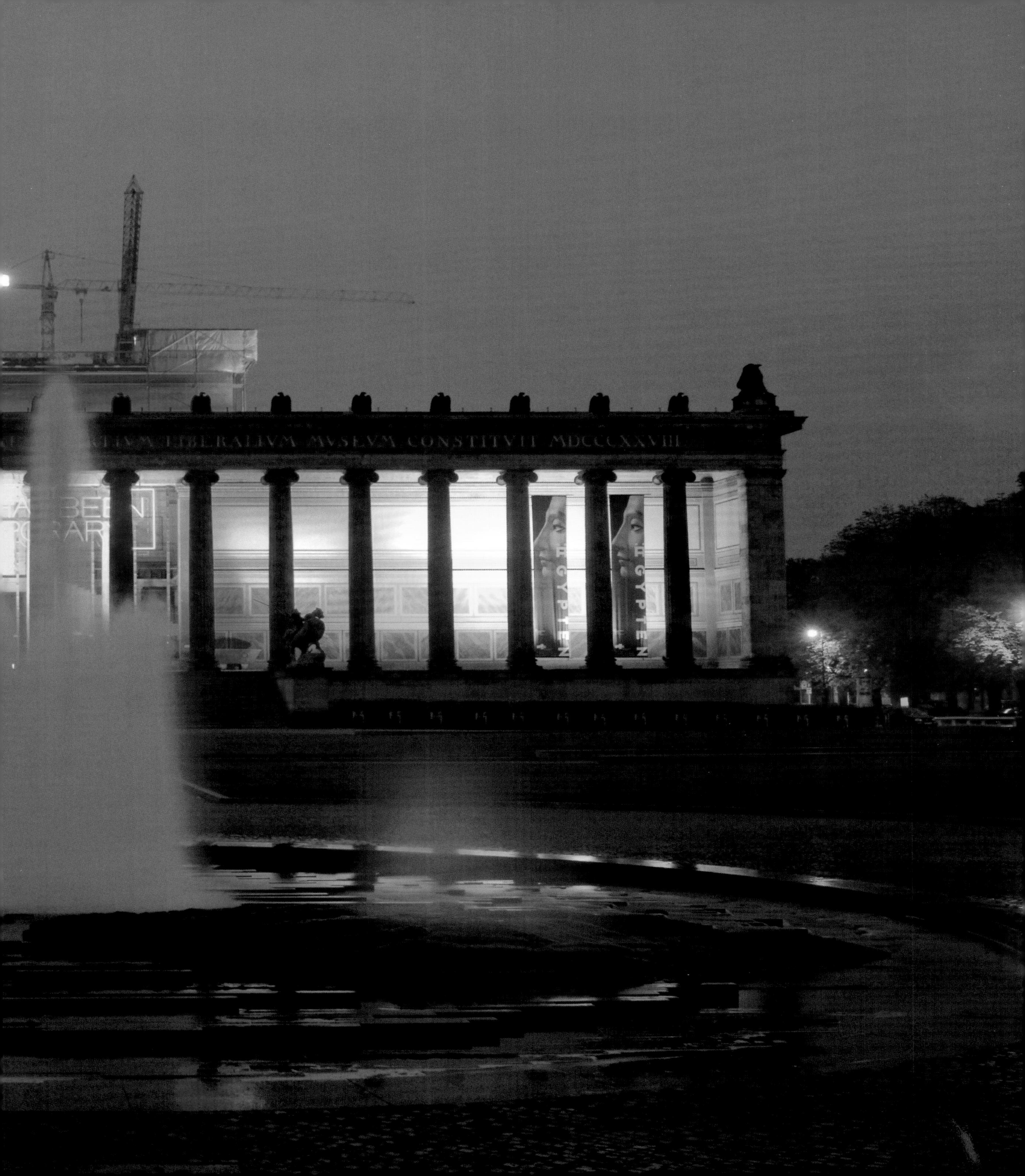

INDEX

© 2007 daab
cologne london new york

published and distributed worldwide by
daab gmbh
friesenstr. 50
d-50670 köln

p + 49 - 221 - 913 927 0
f + 49 - 221 - 913 927 20

mail@daab-online.com
www.daab-online.com

publisher ralf daab
rdaab@daab-online.com

creative director feyyaz
mail@feyyaz.com

© 2007 edited and produced by fusion publishing gmbh stuttgart . los angeles
www.fusion-publishing.com

team: ingo schraut (editor, text introduction), katharina feuer (editorial assistance, layout),
elke roberta buscher (text projects), jan hausberg, martin herterich (imaging & prepress), alphagriese
(translations)

photo credits
coverphoto facts+fiction
introduction page 9 frank rümmele, 11 steffen wirtgen, 13 facts+fiction

printed in poland by ctp ozgraf

isbn 978-3-86654-006-4